Also by Shivi Ramoutar

The Ice Kitchen:
Fast Fresh Food to Fill Your Family and Your Freezer

Cook Clever:
One Chop, No Waste, All Taste

Kris Kirkham

Many moons ago, Shivi Ramoutar was born in Trinidad into a colourful (in all senses of the word) family, and she was brought up between those beloved salty beaches, the grassy Leicestershire countryside (via a brief stint in the Big Apple) and the eclectic buzz of London, where she has now settled and which she calls 'home'. She left a career in law to pursue her passion for food. Her favourite pastimes are tinkling the ivories (her ambition was once to be a classical pianist), writing songs and tap dancing. She lives with her husband and her three little wildlings in a house of utter chaos.

The *Guardian* dubbed her a 'Caribbean Food Supremo', while British Airways' *The Club* magazine calls her the 'Queen of Contemporary Caribbean Cooking', and she has shared her unique, fresh and colourful approach to flavoursome Caribbean food across London and the UK, via her supper club and then subsequently through restaurant and brand collaborations, as well as in various national publications.

Shivi can regularly be found cooking her tropical fare on TV, appearing in her own series, *Jimmy and Shivi's Farmhouse Breakfast*, which airs on Saturday mornings on ITV, as well as on *Saturday Kitchen, James Martin's Saturday Mornings* and *This Morning*.

Shivi is also a passionate spokesperson for promoting tourism in the Caribbean at Caribbean events for both travel and food publications throughout the UK.

https://www.shiviramoutar.com/
Follow Shivi on Instagram @shiviramoutar

RECIPES FROM THE RUM ISLANDS

FOOD & STORIES FROM THE CARIBBEAN

Shivi Ramoutar

Copyright © Shivi Ramoutar 2015
Illustrations © Tola Adaja 2026

The right of Shivi Ramoutar to be identified as the Author of
the Work has been asserted by her in accordance with the
Copyright, Designs and Patents Act 1988.

First published as a full-colour cookbook titled *Caribbean Modern* in 2015 by Headline Home
An imprint of Headline Publishing Group Limited

This reissue edition first published in Hardback in 2026 by Headline Home
An imprint of Headline Publishing Group

1

Apart from any use permitted under UK copyright law, this publication may
only be reproduced, stored, or transmitted, in any form, or by any means, with prior
permission in writing of the publishers or, in the case of reprographic production,
in accordance with the terms of licences issued by the Copyright Licensing Agency.

Cataloguing in Publication Data is available from the British Library

Hardback ISBN 978 1 0354 3428 2
ebook ISBN 978 1 0354 3569 2

Typeset in 10.75/16pt Lyon Text by Six Red Marbles UK, Thetford, Norfolk

Printed and bound in Great Britain by Clays Ltd, Elcograf S.p.A.

Headline's policy is to use papers that are natural, renewable and recyclable
products and made from wood grown in well-managed forests and other
controlled sources. The logging and manufacturing processes are expected
to conform to the environmental regulations of the country of origin.

Headline Publishing Group Limited
An Hachette UK Company
Carmelite House
50 Victoria Embankment
London EC4Y 0DZ

The authorised representative in the EEA is Hachette Ireland,
8 Castlecourt Centre, Dublin 15, D15 XTP3, Ireland (email: info@hbgi.ie)

www.headline.co.uk
www.hachette.co.uk

For Ma and Pa.

Thank you for Roald Dahl's *Revolting Recipes*, for putting up with the blue eggs and other kooky creations that I forced down your throat and for never complaining about the bomb site that I'd leave behind in the kitchen. For everything, I am eternally grateful.

Contents

Introduction 1
Caribbean Food and its Roots 3
My Caribbean Kitchen 8
Notes on the Recipes 10

CUTTERS (SNACKS FOR SHARING)
15

SOUPS & SALADS
42

ONE POT
79

TWO POTS OR THREE
106

SOMETHING ON THE SIDE
139

SWEET THINGS
162

STICKY-FINGERED GOODIES
205

DRINK UP
226

FOR THE LARDER
243

Acknowledgements 283

Index 285

Introduction

I find it quite astonishing that when the word 'Caribbean' is mentioned, a hundred beautiful clichés bubble to the surface: white sand, blue sky, crystalline water, sea-salt breezes, sticky days, balmy nights, palm-fringed shores, rum-laced cocktails ... And yet, when the words 'Caribbean' and 'food' are thrown together in a sentence, the first thing that generally springs to mind is the stereotypical 'Jerk Chicken, Rice and Peas'. (Mutton Curry usually comes in second and there is normally a struggle to think of a third!) I am not certain how this particular dish has become representative of Caribbean cuisine – and, don't get me wrong, it is utterly moreish – but there are so many other tantalising treats that deserve to battle it out for centre stage among the flamboyant islands known as the Caribbean.

What exactly comprises the Caribbean is a moot point. Geographically, it can be classified as the thousand-odd islands in the Caribbean Sea and the surrounding coastal territories, tucked in between the American continents and east of Central America. Culturally, it is a melting pot of various identities – East Indian, West African, Chinese, European, American and the indigenous Amerindians – that together represent what is now the Caribbean identity. With such wide-ranging ethnic influences, the Caribbean is flamboyant, vibrant and colourful.

Food is at the heart of Caribbean life. No matter how many people turn up at a home here – and no matter what the hour – someone will always gravitate towards the kitchen to whip up some food. I have vivid memories of my childhood in Trinidad, growing up in a mixed Caribbean/South American/Indian family where life was bustling and there were always plenty of people – friends, family, tag-alongs – around. There was always more than enough food for everyone, and yet not a single scrap remained by the time the last person left. Nothing ever went to waste!

Laughter was one of the most familiar sounds. Whether sunshine was streaming in or hot rain was pelting down, there was always a reason to laugh, to drink rum, to play cricket in the streets and to 'lime' (see page 13). This hasn't changed over the years: even now when I go back to visit family, it is like everyone has a revolving door and the kitchen is always full to bursting with friends. Social cooking, eating and spontaneous hospitality feel as natural to us Caribbeans as our own heartbeat.

Outside of the home, too, the Caribbean has one of the most vibrant and varied street-food scenes that I have ever come across, with vendors selling from stalls on street corners, out of the back of vans in car parks and at beach shacks – a clear indication of how much our lives revolve around our stomachs!

Caribbean Food and its Roots

I am often asked what exactly is Caribbean cuisine? What are its defining flavours, influences and origins? What is it about the range of dishes that gives Caribbean cuisine its unique identity?

Usually, the concept of 'identity' implies an obvious unifying factor. If you think about Indian, Chinese or Italian food, it seems quite obvious, doesn't it? But with Caribbean food, the unifying factor is diversity – at its most extreme. We Caribbean folk have a huge variety of origins, religions and colours. You only need to look at my family to see what I mean: our different skin and eye colours reflect our indigenous, Indian, South American, Hispanic and even Asian ancestry. (I can't imagine where I'd end up if I were to trace my family tree!) The Caribbean can be seen as one of the first multicultural societies in existence due to its colourful history and the continuous 'musical chairs' of colonists throughout the islands, all of which have influenced Caribbean food and ways of eating.

If we were to go on a little food tour of the Caribbean, you would quickly discover how each island differs from its neighbours. Jamaica is known for its jerk, ackee and saltfish as well as its patties (see page 121). Jerk (see page 273) was inspired by the African slaves who came to Jamaica with a method of heavily spicing pork and cooking it over hot coals to preserve the meat. The runaway slaves adopted this method and used the vegetation and spices found in the mountains to preserve wild boar, as often they didn't know when they would next eat! The method has continued to evolve over the centuries into the jerk we now know and love. Patties were inspired by the British, who brought with them recipes for pasties, amongst other things.

Hopping over to Guyana, we meet the famous Caribbean one-pot dish, Lamb Pepperpot (see page 96), derived from local Amerindian ancestry, as well as a host of Caribbean–Chinese mash-up meals that emerged from the mass influx of indentured Chinese servants mixing their traditional food with Caribbean flavours.

Leaping north to the Bahamas, the array of chowders (see my Shellfish Chowder, page 103), crayfish salads and grits point to the Deep South as the main influence, with South America having inspired ceviche (see my Mock Conch Salad, page 76).

The lovely little haven that is Curaçao still exhibits the influence of its principal colonists, the Dutch, in local dishes, such as the tasty little dumplings called oliebollen, amongst other Creole food (krioyo), which evolved from the African–European ancestry.

Trinidad is another example of this melting-pot syndrome, with Persian-originated Pelau, Indian-derived Roti, fried chicken from the Deep South and the South American-influenced Pasteles (see pages 81, 149, 116 and 109), to name just a few. Here, flavours have evolved, using local produce, to create dishes that are familiar and yet quite different.

So how did all this variety come about? Way before the fifteenth century and the arrival of the Europeans, the Caribbean was inhabited by indigenous groups: foraging American–Indian nomads from Central America who were followed by agriculturalists from South America. Their diet was mostly made up of vegetables and fruit, such as peanuts, guava, papaya, cassava (a starchy root vegetable), cocoa and pineapples. Additionally, they were reliant on fish (and were skilled fishermen) and hunted small mammals (some similar to guinea pigs), turtles, lizards and birds (there are no large species of animal native to the Caribbean). The practice of using hot chilli peppers to spice food is thought to have started at this time and has continued. The indigenous people can also be credited with inventing one of the first barbecue techniques known to man, making 'grills' (barbacoa) out of green wood (green to prevent burning) over a fire, on which they would slow-cook meats.

The colonial era of the Caribbean began soon after Christopher Columbus's voyages to the Americas in the late 1400s and early 1500s, with Spain being the main colonial power. The Spaniards introduced sugar cane (which was found to make rum and which became the key crop cultivated in the Caribbean, giving rise to the plantation system that dictated much of the area's history), as well as much vegetation now referred to as 'tropical', including ginger, figs, bananas, plantain, grapes, oranges, limes, onion, garlic, chickpeas and – surprising to some – coconuts. They also brought with them cattle, pigs, goats and chickens. With the arrival of the conquistadors, the indigenous people were captured, enslaved and nearly wiped out (not only by forced labour and war, but also by diseases introduced from Europe). Soon after the Spanish had settled, the Portuguese, English, French, Danish and Dutch arrived, bringing their own culinary techniques and ingredients, including coffee, black pepper, mangoes (from Asia), methods for salting cod (bacalao), sweet pudding recipes, souse and black pudding (the latter, in particular, became a much-loved Caribbean food, see my Scallop, Puddin' and Sour, page 47).

During the 1600s, as the enslaved indigenous population dwindled, the European colonists turned to the slave trade for the mass manpower required to support the sugar plantation systems across the Caribbean. As well as slaves, the colonists brought back from Africa yam (a root vegetable), okra, black eye peas, callaloo (a leafy plant) and ackee (a fruit).

The slaves were usually given a small piece of land, generally of poor quality, on which to grow their own food crops, which included sweet potatoes, yams and other 'ground provisions', in addition to plantain and the measly rations of salted meat or lacklustre leftovers with which the plantation owners would provide them. Thus these foods became stigmatised as 'slave' foods that the Europeans would not eat themselves. Nowadays, however, they are very much a commonplace staple within the Caribbean diet and immensely enjoyed by all.

The slaves also developed a method of cooking that is still evident in the modern Caribbean kitchen. Due to limited and poor-quality cooking utensils – normally no more than an iron pot, a wooden spoon and a pestle and mortar – and the need for making food as hearty as possible, the 'one-pot' meal emerged. All the ingredients would be cooked up together and made incredibly thick. As ground provisions or leftovers could be bland, and were sometimes even going off, meals were heavily seasoned with an array of herbs and spices and meat was marinated, not only to enhance flavours but also to disguise unpleasant ones. This influence is strongly evident in many Caribbean dishes.

Once slavery was abolished in the 1800s, the Europeans brought indentured servants from China and India as a new form of cheap labour to work the plantations. At first the

Chinese couldn't prepare their native dishes because they couldn't get hold of their traditional ingredients, but they did make noodles. Eventually they were able to bring across spices, soy sauce and then rice and mustard, but the Chinese influence on Caribbean cuisine really became evident only during the twentieth century when these ingredients arrived.

The Indians brought curry recipes (which they adapted to take into account the ingredients available in the Caribbean), roti (a very popular flatbread) and eating meals on banana leaves, a custom that is still prevalent in some homes and restaurants in the Caribbean. As you will see from my recipes, Indian food has had an important influence on Caribbean cuisine.

During the last century, with the dawn of television, ease of travel and our natural, human inquisitiveness, the influence of the rest of the world on the Caribbean has become evident in the proliferation of fast-food outlets (fried chicken being one of the most popular) and the range of ingredients and products available to buy in the supermarkets. We Caribbeans like to dabble in all these other-worldy flavours, trying them in their original state and then doing what we do best: reinterpreting dishes to make them our own.

My Caribbean Kitchen

The recipes in this book are my own interpretation of the Caribbean flavours, cooking and eating experiences that have shaped my life. They are a reflection of how I eat and cook at home: sometimes light and fresh, sometimes heavier, with a little more effort needed, but always satisfyingly homely and hearty food with all the excitement and exotic flavour of a faraway place.

I am very conscious of what I eat, and all the rapidly evolving guidelines on plant points, gut food, variety of produce, etc, but I do love my food. I love to try new flavours, I also love traditional dishes, and I have come to realise that I have an insatiable sweet tooth, so I have tried to balance this book in the same way. I've translated age-old, local recipes into fresh, easy and contemporary ones, which will bring the essence of the Caribbean into your home, via day-to-day meals but also more extravagant feasts. The recipes range from Caribbean interpretations of well-loved and familiar foods to simplified Westernised versions of classic Caribbean dishes, substituting ingredients that you will easily find in your local supermarket where appropriate. I want to show you the versatility of both tropical and local British produce and how you can use them together to create some really special dishes.

And ingredients? I like food preparation and the sourcing of ingredients to be as easy and enjoyable as sitting down to eat a meal, so you won't find particular Caribbean ingredients – for example breadfruit, plantain or chataigne – listed here. As delicious as these are, I have had to adapt my way of cooking to take account of British produce and the fact that it isn't always easy to find some of these far-flung ingredients, especially if I want to whip up something exotic at short notice. That said, however, it is now common for high-street supermarkets to stock the ingredients – or more than ample substitutes – you will need to recreate absolutely any dish from the Islands.

And so I am happy to present you with this colourful collection of fresh and easy recipes, inspired by the Caribbean approach to cooking (and eating) and by its wealth of flavours and ingredients. I hope that this book will bring a little bit of the tropics into your kitchen and on to your table and that it will encourage you to create sun-drenched recipes of your own.

Notes on the Recipes

These recipes are to inspire you, so feel free to add or replace ingredients and to develop the recipes as you wish.

- All temperatures are listed for a conventional oven. If you are using a fan-assisted oven, reduce the temperature by 20°C.
- When pumpkin is out of season, or difficult to get a hold of, feel free to substitute butternut squash.
- My 'go-to' cooking oil is olive oil, but use whatever you prefer.
- For deep-frying, or high temperature cooking, I use peanut (or groundnut) oil as it is flavourless and has a high smoking point, so doesn't burn easily. Sunflower or vegetable oil makes a good substitute, though.
- For stock, any good-quality, ideally fresh, or store-bought variety will be fine.
- Onions and garlic are considered peeled unless otherwise stated.
- Unless otherwise stated, butter can be salted or unsalted.
- If possible, use free-range eggs.
- Feel free to swap brown rice for white rice and vice versa; just make sure that you adjust the cooking time as brown rice takes much longer to cook than white.
- My go-to tamarind concentrate is Natco (available at supermarkets and online). If you can't find this, don't worry, but try to use a concentrate, or paste that is thick, rather than a heavily diluted version.
- When working with hot chillies, wear gloves (or rub your fingers first with a little cooking oil) to protect your skin, and

wash your hands, the chopping board and the knife thoroughly afterwards.
- The easiest and least wasteful way to peel ginger and turmeric is by using a spoon, angled towards you, to gently scrape away the skin.
- Before juicing citrus fruits, roll them firmly on a hard surface with the palm of your hand a few times to release the fibres and therefore more juice.
- Cracking a fresh coconut can sometimes be a little tricky. You need first to pierce the 'eyes' and 'mouth' at the end of the coconut and allow any milk to drain off (this isn't coconut water and, although it can be used in recipes, it tastes a little 'off'). Pop the drained coconut into a bag and, on a hard surface (the kitchen floor), using a hammer and a little 'spirit', smash the coconut. Remove the coconut from the bag and carefully, using a sharp knife, prise apart the hard shell from the nut. The brown skin remaining on the nut is absolutely fine to eat, but you can peel this away with a potato peeler, if you wish.
- I strongly suggest that the rum you use for the recipes is dark rum of good quality. This will give your dishes complexity and spiced mellowness rather than that horrid sharp alcohol taste that you get when using cheaper bottles. As most of the recipes that use rum require only a small amount of the tipple, it's definitely worth spending just that little bit more on a bottle and keeping it for when needed (and for enjoying the odd sip in the evening).
- Angostura Bitters, from Trinidad, is renowned in the cocktail world and is made from botanical aromatic ingredients. It acts as a phenomenal flavour-enhancer not only in drinks but

also in food. There is alcohol in the bitters, which acts as a solvent and a preservative, but as you tend to use only the odd dash in the recipes, the alcoholic content added is insignificant.

- Sterilise your jars and bottles by washing them on the hottest setting in the dishwasher. Alternatively, you can place washed jars upside-down on a baking sheet in an oven preheated to 160°C/Gas 3 for 15 minutes. It is best to fill the jars when they are still hot. Pop wax discs on to the still warm surface of jams, pickles and preserves to lengthen their shelf life.

A Note on 'Liming'

This has nothing to do with the green-skinned citrus fruit, but rather is a wonderful cultural phenomenon, originating in Trinidad, that has been defined as 'the art of doing nothing'. It isn't a party, it isn't idle laziness, but rather it's purposeful chilling out, letting the world go by, usually with a glass of rum in hand, food in close proximity (i.e. in the other hand) and laughter and conversation flowing.

CUTTERS
(SNACKS FOR SHARING)

CUTTERS

(LYDIAN, FOR MARTIN)

Choka

SERVES 4–8

Choka, taken from our Indian heritage, is a generic word for vegetables that have been roasted and then crushed. It's as simple as it sounds and gives you the most full-bodied, tasty and healthy dips! Not only do I whip this up and serve it with warm pitta bread or flatbread as a nibble for peckish friends, I also make it regularly for 'Meatless Monday' dinners to eat with Fried Bakes (see page 141) or Buss-Up Shut (see page 149) – just like my grandmother, Mama, would make us for breakfast.

TIME: 5 MINUTES PREP + 15 MINUTES COOKING

For the baigan choka
3 large aubergines
3 garlic cloves, smashed
3 tbsp extra virgin olive oil
generous pinch of cayenne pepper, plus extra for garnishing
½ tsp finely chopped flat-leaf parsley leaves

For the tomato choka
6 overripe tomatoes
¼ onion, finely chopped
1½ tbsp finely chopped coriander leaves
3 tbsp extra virgin olive oil

3 large garlic cloves, crushed
sea salt and freshly ground black pepper

1. Heat a griddle pan on a high heat.
2. To make the baigan choka, use the tip of a sharp knife to slash a deep 2cm-long line in each aubergine and stuff the smashed garlic deep inside the slash.
3. When the griddle pan is smoking, pop the aubergines on and cook for about 8–10 minutes, turning regularly, until all sides are blackened and blistered and the aubergines are soft and tender. Remove the aubergines and set aside to cool.
4. In the meantime, pop the tomatoes for the tomato choka on to the griddle pan and cook for about 3–5 minutes, turning regularly, until blackened and blistered. Remove the tomatoes and set aside to cool.
5. To finish the baigan choka, cut off the stems, peel the skins from the aubergines and discard the crushed garlic. In a large bowl using a fork, crush the aubergines, along with the oil, until of a chunky consistency. Add the cayenne pepper, stir well and season to taste. Serve in a small bowl, sprinkling over a little cayenne pepper and the chopped parsley.
6. Remove any stems from the tomatoes and peel off the blackened skin. In a large bowl, crush the tomatoes with a potato masher or a fork and add the chopped onion and coriander.
7. To finish the tomato choka, heat the oil in a small frying pan on a medium heat and fry the garlic until it starts to turn gold, about 30 seconds or so, stirring continuously, then remove from the heat and tip the oil with the crushed

garlic into the crushed tomato. The choka will be runny with some chunks of tomato. Mix well and season with salt and pepper. Decant into a small serving bowl. Both chokas will keep for up to 3 days in the fridge.

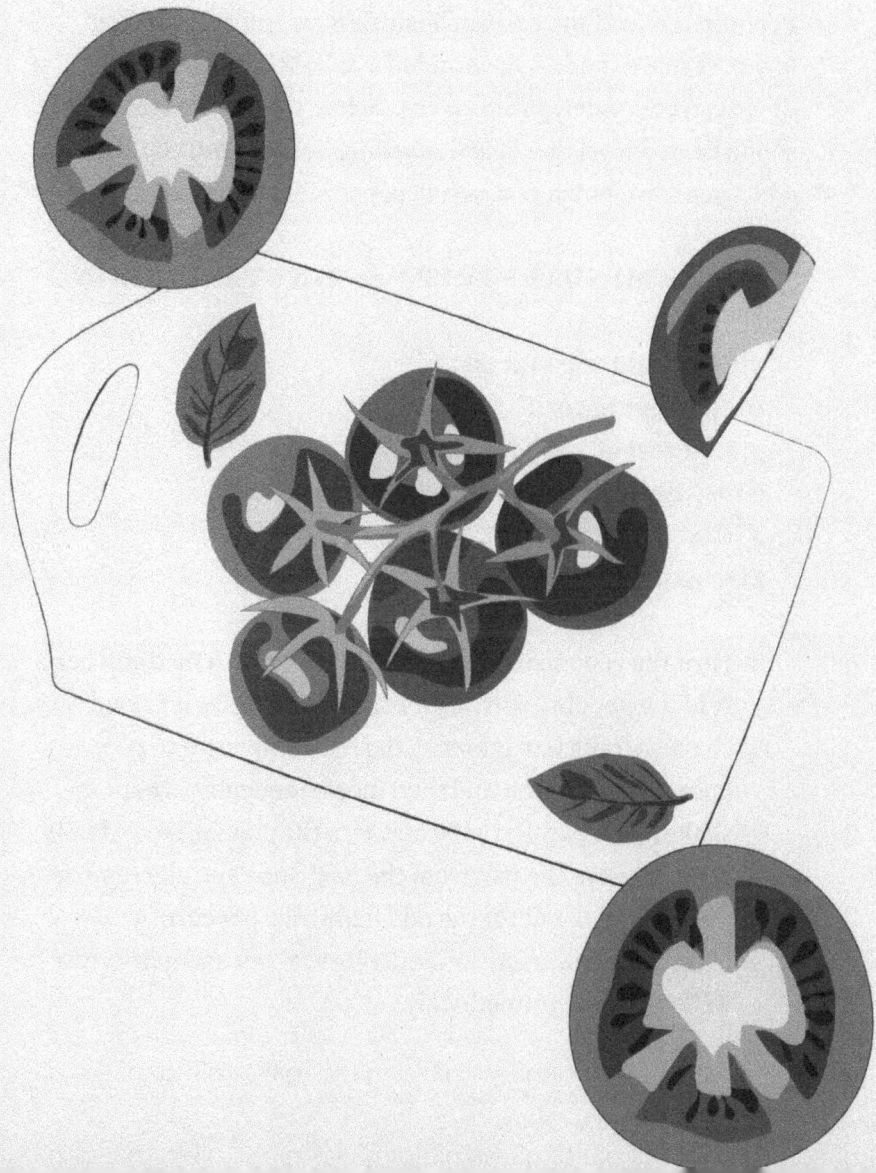

Salt, Lime & Coriander Popcorn

SERVES 6-8

Popcorn is one of the easiest, healthiest and most satisfying low-cost snack foods. I have added a delightful smattering of lime zest, coriander, garlic and a pinch of salt to take it to a more sophisticated level of tropical snacking heaven. You could also add a generous pinch of cayenne pepper for a little extra spice.

TIME: 5 MINUTES PREP + 10 MINUTES COOKING

3 tbsp virgin coconut oil
100g popping corn
grated zest of 4 limes
6 tbsp finely chopped coriander leaves
4 tsp sea salt
2 tsp garlic granules

1. Heat the coconut oil in a large saucepan on a medium heat. Add the popping corn, cover the pan and give it a good shake. After a few minutes, the corn will begin to pop, occasionally at first and then more frequently – keep shaking the pan on the heat. Once the popping sound tails away, remove the pan from the heat and carefully remove the lid. Watch out for the odd kamikaze popcorn!
2. Mix in the lime zest, coriander leaves, salt and garlic, toss well and serve immediately.

Zaboca on Crab Biscotti

SERVES 4-6 (MAKES ABOUT 24 SMALL BISCOTTI)

Zaboca is a local Trinidadian word for avocado. Caribbean avocados are incredible, the size of two fists sometimes and always as creamy as butter. The subtle sweetness of the crab really sings in this easy-to-make biscotti and it goes hand in hand with the avocado. This is a great canapé, works perfectly with a soup at lunchtime or makes a light afternoon nibble.

TIME: 15 MINUTES PREP + 50 MINUTES COOKING

For the biscotti
270g self-raising flour
1½ tbsp mixed dried herbs
25g caster sugar
112g unsalted butter, at room temperature
2 free-range eggs, beaten
80g white crabmeat, flaked
sea salt and freshly ground black pepper

For the zaboca
4 soft, ripe avocados, roughly mashed
4 tbsp extra virgin olive oil
2 garlic cloves, crushed
½ chilli, seeded and finely chopped
juice of 2 limes

1. Pre-heat the oven to 175°C/Gas 4 and line a baking sheet with greaseproof paper.
2. In a small bowl, using a fork, stir together the flour, herbs, a good pinch of salt and a grind of pepper.
3. In a large bowl, use a wooden spoon to cream the sugar and butter, then gradually beat in the beaten egg then the crabmeat.
4. Stir in the flour mixture then use floured hands to bring the dough together into a ball and divide into two. Roll each ball into a long flattened log, about 4cm wide and 2cm high.
5. Place the logs on to the lined baking sheet and bake in the oven for 30 minutes, until just cooked through and firm.
6. Remove the logs from the oven and when they are cool enough to handle, take a serrated knife and gently (as the biscotti is quite crumbly) slice, at a slightly diagonal angle, into 1cm thick slices. Pop the biscotti back on to the lined baking sheet and bake for a further 15–20 minutes, until golden.
7. Meanwhile make the zaboca: in a large bowl mix together the avocado, olive oil, garlic and chilli, adding lime juice and seasoning to taste. It should be a little chunky.
8. Remove the biscotti from the oven and transfer to a wire rack to allow to cool completely. These will keep in an airtight container in the fridge for a couple days.
9. To serve, top the biscotti with the zaboca and eat immediately.

Cornmeal Baked Okra

SERVES 6

Okra is a versatile little vegetable that crops up in many a Caribbean dish: it is great in curry, pan-fried with garlic and onion, and is a key ingredient in Cou-cou, a wet cornmeal dish. I know that the slightly mucus-y nature of the seeds can be a bit much for some people. If you're one of them, try this light, healthy recipe: here the baking and encasing in a crunchy, cornmeal-based seasoning seems to balance that. This is a great nibble, best served with a good blob of Pineapple Ketchup (see page 262).

TIME: 5 MINUTES PREP + 20 MINUTES COOKING

175g okra, stems removed
150ml buttermilk
olive oil, to drizzle

For the cornmeal crust
100g fine cornmeal
3 thyme sprigs, leaves only, finely chopped
1–2½ tsp paprika (depending on how spicy you want it)
1 heaped tsp sea salt
¼–½ tsp chilli powder (depending on how spicy you want it)

¼ tsp freshly ground black pepper
¼ tsp ground cumin

1. Pre-heat the oven to 200°C/Gas 6.
2. To make the crust, mix together all the ingredients in a large freezer bag.
3. Put the okra into a small bowl and pour over the buttermilk, ensuring that the okra is fully coated.
4. Use a slotted spoon to transfer the buttermilk-coated okra into the freezer bag containing the cornmeal crust mix, allowing any excess buttermilk to drip back into the bowl. Tie the top of the freezer bag, allowing room in the bag to shake it and turn it upside down to fully coat the okra in the crust.
5. Tip the okra out on to a baking sheet and drizzle generously with olive oil. Pop in the oven and bake for about 20 minutes, until golden brown, crisp and cooked through. Eat immediately.

Baked Split Peas

SERVES 4-8

These crunchy little things, sold in supermarkets (and at stalls en route to beaches) in large plastic bottles, are one of the tastiest, easy-to-make snacks and are a healthy alternative to crisps. Adapt the quantities of spices to suit your taste and add other flavourings if you fancy: try dried mixed herbs and garlic, or cumin and curry powder. You can also make a no-soak version using canned chickpeas: drain them, spice them and bake for a little longer, until crispy.

TIME: OVERNIGHT SOAKING + 5 MINUTES PREP + 30 MINUTES COOKING

500g yellow split peas
1 tbsp bicarbonate of soda
4 tbsp olive oil
2 tbsp chilli powder
1 tbsp paprika
1 tbsp garlic granules
1 tbsp sea salt
½ tbsp black pepper

1. Tip the split peas into a large bowl, sprinkle over the bicarbonate of soda and cover with cold water. Leave to soak overnight.

2. The next day, pre-heat the oven to 170°C/Gas 3.
3. Drain the split peas, put them into a sieve and rinse under cold running water then pat them dry with kitchen paper.
4. Pop them into a large bowl, add the oil, chilli powder, paprika, garlic granules, salt and pepper and mix well to coat.
5. Empty the split peas out on to a few large baking sheets: if possible the split peas should be in a single layer. Pop the trays into the oven and bake for about 25–30 minutes, until the peas are golden and lightly toasted, stirring them every 5–10 minutes and swapping the trays around in the oven to ensure that they cook evenly.
6. As they cool they will continue to crisp up. Allow to cool completely, then store in an airtight container for up to 5 days.

Spice-Crust Squid & Lemon 'Aïoli'

SERVES 6-8

One of my more recent memories of Tobago is of sitting outdoors for dinner, near Grafton Beach, hearing the waves roaring in the near distance and enjoying (or, if I'm honest, inhaling) a platter of crispy squid. The two things that make this dish are the seasoning and keeping the squid tender; you really don't want to overcook it. I have used cornflour rather than plain flour because it makes for a thin and super crisp crust. For a veggie-friendly version, replace the squid with finger-sized, sturdy veg (e.g. aubergines, courgettes, mushrooms and peppers).

TIME: 2 HOURS SOAKING + 10 MINUTES PREP + 15 MINUTES COOKING

500g squid, cleaned and cut into 0.5–1cm-thick rings (do not discard the tentacles)
500ml whole milk
groundnut oil, for deep frying
1 lemon, quartered, to serve

For the spice crust
250g cornflour
3 tsp paprika
1 tsp chilli powder

1½ tsp ground cumin
1½ tsp garlic granules
1 tsp cayenne pepper
½ tsp ground coriander
1 heaped tsp sea salt
½ tsp freshly ground black pepper

For the lemon 'aïoli'
6 tbsp mayonnaise
6 large garlic cloves, crushed
1 lemon, zest and juice
sea salt and freshly ground black pepper

1. Put the squid into a large bowl and pour over the milk, ensuring that the squid is fully submerged. Place in the fridge for 2 hours.
2. To make the spice crust, use a fork to stir together all the ingredients in a large bowl.
3. To make the lemon 'aïoli', whisk together all the ingredients until smooth and season to taste. Keep in the fridge until 20 minutes before serving, then let it sit out at room temperature.
4. Pour the oil into a large wok, or high-sided saucepan, so that it comes halfway up. (If using a deep-fat fryer, follow the manufacturer's guidelines.) Heat the oil to 180°C: when you pop a breadcrumb in, it should sizzle and turn golden brown almost immediately. Prepare a bowl, lined with kitchen paper, and set this down near the wok.
5. In the meantime, remove the squid from the milk and pat dry lightly with kitchen paper to absorb any excess milk.

Toss the squid in the spice crust mixture, ensuring that every ring and tentacle is fully coated in the seasoning.

6. Working in batches, pop the squid into the oil and fry for 1½–3 minutes until crisp and very lightly golden. Remove with a slotted spoon and tip into the lined bowl to absorb any excess oil. Repeat with the remaining squid.
7. Put all the squid on to a serving platter along with the lemon quarters and serve with the lemon 'aïoli'.

'Paradise' Prawns

SERVES 4–6

The combination of classic Indo-Caribbean spicing, the charred, sweet succulence of griddled prawns and the light coconut oil and garlic dressing is enough to make me suffer the consequences of my shellfish allergy and tuck right in. As well as being an easy-to-prepare, healthy dinner-party snack or sharing plate, this also works as a quick mid-week dinner with a chunk of soft bread or a green salad. Paradise on a plate has never been simpler!

TIME: 5 MINUTES PREP + 20 MINUTES MARINATING + 3 MINUTES COOKING

16 raw jumbo prawns, peeled and veins removed but with heads and tails left on
½ tbsp chopped coriander leaves
sea salt and freshly ground black pepper

for the wet rub
2 tsp olive oil
1 heaped tsp amchar masala spice mix (see page 279)
scant pinch of ground turmeric

for the dressing
2 tbsp virgin coconut oil

2 garlic cloves, crushed
zest of ½ lime

1. To make the wet rub, mix together all the ingredients with a pinch of salt. Rub into the prepared prawns, ensuring that all are well coated, and leave to marinate in the fridge for at least 20 minutes before cooking, then thread the prawns on to four metal or wooden skewers.
2. In the meantime, heat a griddle pan on a high heat.
3. For the dressing, melt the coconut oil in a small frying pan on a low heat, then add the garlic and sauté for about 30 seconds, until the gorgeous garlicky aroma hits you.
4. Remove the pan from the heat and stir in the lime zest, season to taste and keep warm.
5. When the griddle pan is smoking hot, add the prawns and cook for about 2 minutes on each side until just cooked through and charred on the outside.
6. Toss the prawns in the dressing, tip it all out into a serving bowl, scatter the coriander over and serve immediately.

For the barbecue
If you are using wooden skewers, ensure that they have been soaked in cold water for an hour or so before cooking. Pre-heat the barbecue until the coals have just turned white. Pop the prepared prawn skewers on to the hottest part of the barbecue and cook for about 2–3 minutes on each side, until just cooked through and charred on the outside. Serve as above.

Shrimp & Black Bean Fritters with Tamarind Dip

I know that fritters can sometimes have the reputation of being heavy, but I find this crushed black bean filling, brimming with a subtle and fresh shrimp sweetness, makes for a lighter treat. The sharp and spicy tamarind dip is the perfect accompaniment. Enjoy as a snack, or have four or five (or more!) with a green salad for a light lunch or dinner.

MAKES ABOUT 12 FRITTERS

TIME: 10 MINUTES PREP + 15 MINUTES COOKING

For the shrimp and black bean fritters
180g canned black beans, drained, roughly crushed with the back of a fork
180g raw prawns, peeled, veins removed, and finely chopped
1½ tbsp finely chopped coriander leaves
1½ spring onions, finely chopped
1½ tsp Pepper Sauce (see page 258), or ¾ chilli, seeded and finely chopped
1½ garlic cloves, crushed
60g self-raising flour
½ tsp baking powder
15g panko breadcrumbs
1½ tsp paprika
1½ tsp celery salt
2 free-range eggs, beaten

3 tbsp water
groundnut oil, for deep-frying
sea salt and freshly ground black pepper

For the tamarind dip
2 tbsp tamarind paste
juice of ½ orange
1 tsp hot sauce (or, a little fingernail-sized piece of Scotch bonnet, seeded and finely chopped)
2 garlic cloves, crushed
1 tbsp finely chopped coriander leaves

1. In a large bowl, mix together all the fritter ingredients except for the eggs, water and oil, adding a small pinch of salt (bear in mind that you have already added celery salt) and a grind of pepper. Once everything is well mixed, add the beaten egg and slowly trickle in the water, stirring regularly, until you have a thick batter, of dropping consistency (you may not need to use all the water so add it very gradually).
2. Pour the oil into a large wok, or high-sided saucepan, so that it comes halfway up. (If using a deep-fat fryer, follow the manufacturer's guidelines.) Heat the oil to 180°C: when you pop a breadcrumb in it should sizzle and turn golden brown almost immediately. Line a large plate with kitchen paper and set this down near the wok.
3. To make the tamarind dip, whisk together the tamarind paste, orange juice and Pepper Sauce in a small bowl until smooth. Pour 2 teaspoons of this liquid into a mortar, add the garlic and coriander leaves (and the Scotch bonnet, if

you are using it) and, using a pestle, bash and smoosh together with a pinch of salt until you have a smooth paste. Add the paste to the tamarind and orange mixture and whisk until combined. Season to taste.

4. To cook the fritters, using two tablespoons, take a spoonful of the fritter batter and roughly shape into a ball a little smaller than a golf ball by passing it, and shaping it, between the two spoons. Drop the fritter batter into the oil and fry for about 4 minutes, until golden brown and cooked through (a skewer inserted into the centre should come out clean), then remove with a slotted spoon and place the cooked fritters on to the lined plate. You can fry about 4 fritters at the same time, depending on the size of your pan. Don't overcrowd the pan though, otherwise the temperature of the oil will drop and the fritters will end up soggy and oily.

5. Transfer the fritters to a serving plate and serve with the tamarind dip alongside.

Aubergine Croquettes

In the Caribbean, we have many names for aubergine, including 'baigan' and 'boulanger', but whatever you call it, I'm obsessed with it! It is such a 'meaty' veg, that it can make a filling meal all on its own. When my sisters and I were kids with the 'afternoon munchies', my pa would often whip up breadcrumbed and baked aubergine slices from his magically unending snack repertoire. So this recipe is in homage to him and his aubergine snack. If you don't want to fry these, you can also bake them on a high heat, just make sure that the croquettes are well drizzled with oil so that they become golden and crispy. This tastes great with a spoonful of Yellow Pepper Jam (see page 256).

MAKES ABOUT 16 CROQUETTES

TIME: 10 MINUTES PREP + 25 MINUTES COOKING

2 large aubergines
10g butter
1 large spring onion, finely chopped
½ tbsp finely chopped flat-leaf parsley
2 garlic cloves, crushed
200g panko breadcrumbs
½ tsp cayenne pepper
1 tsp paprika
½ tsp celery salt
70g gram flour

2 free-range eggs beaten
groundnut oil, for frying
sea salt and freshly ground black pepper

1. Heat a griddle pan on a high heat, until smoking. Pop the aubergines on and cook until blistered and soft all over, about 8–10 minutes, turning regularly. Set aside until cool enough to handle then cut the stems off the aubergines and peel away and discard the skin.
2. In a large bowl, blitz the aubergines with a stick blender until smooth. Stir in the butter, spring onion, parsley, garlic, 120g of the panko breadcrumbs, the cayenne pepper, paprika and celery salt. Mix well and season to taste.
3. Scoop a large tablespoon of the mixture and use your hands to form it into a small sphere, then flatten it with your fingers into a round croquette about 5cm wide and 1cm deep. Set aside and repeat with the remaining aubergine mix.
4. Now prepare a production line of a bowl containing the gram flour, a second containing the beaten egg, a third containing the remaining 80g of panko breadcrumbs and a large plate or tray.
5. Carefully dunk a croquette into the gram flour, then the egg, then the breadcrumbs, ensuring that it is fully coated, then set aside on the plate. Continue with the remaining croquettes. A trick here is to use one hand for the dry ingredients and the other hand for the aubergine mix and the egg. (You can prepare the recipe up to this stage in advance and store in the fridge for up to 3 days, or freeze for up to 2 months. Defrost thoroughly before cooking.)

6. In a large wok, or high-sided saucepan, pour the oil in so that it comes one third of the way up. (If using a deep-fat fryer, follow the manufacturer's guidelines.) Heat the oil to 180°C: when you pop a breadcrumb in it should sizzle and turn golden brown almost immediately. Place a plate or tray lined with a few sheets of kitchen paper close to the wok.
7. Fry the croquettes in batches until golden, then set aside on the lined plate to soak up any excess oil. Continue with the remaining croquettes then serve.

Cheese 'Rotsties'

SERVES 3-6

This Trinidadian breakfast street food is really called 'Pepper Roti', but I like calling it 'rotstie' because of its similarity to a cheese toastie (or a quesadilla). The roti isn't just stuffed with grilled cheese, though: the herby, chilli-laced potato filling rockets this to another level of 'toastie', and you can add sliced mushrooms or shreds of ham or anything else you fancy too. It makes a great TV snack, a light dinner with a little salad or a cracking weekend brunch dish with a fried egg on top.

TIME: 30 MINUTES PREP + 45 MINUTES RESTING + 40 MINUTES COOKING

450g self-raising flour, sifted plus extra for dusting
2 tsp sea salt
270ml water
olive oil, for rubbing
45g ghee, melted

For the filling
3 new potatoes (approx. 150g), peeled
¼ onion, finely chopped
2 garlic cloves, crushed
½ red pepper, seeded and roughly chopped
1 red chilli, stem removed, seeded and roughly chopped

½ tbsp coriander leaves, roughly chopped
½ tbsp chopped chives
100g Gruyère, Jarlsberg or Emmental, grated
150g mature Cheddar, grated
sea salt and freshly ground black pepper

1. In a large bowl using a fork, mix together the flour and salt until well combined. Little by little, add the water, using a wooden spoon to stir until a dough forms and comes together in a ball. You may not need to use all the water, so do pour it in gradually. The dough should be soft, but not sticky. If it is a little sticky, add a little more flour.
2. Rub the palms of your hands with a couple of drops of oil, pat it on to the dough and turn the dough out on to a lightly floured surface. Knead the dough for about 5 minutes, until soft and smooth. Wrap in cling film then leave in a warm place to rest for 30 minutes.
3. Divide the dough into six balls, and on a lightly floured surface, roll one of the dough balls into a 25cm-diameter circle. Using a pastry brush, generously brush the surface of the dough with the ghee (see the pictures overleaf).
4. Using a sharp knife, carefully cut the dough from the centre point out to the edge of the circle in a straight slice. Take the cut edge and roll up, all the way around the dough, so you end up with a cone. Stand the cone upright, like a traffic cone on its head, and flatten it with the palm of your hand. Repeat with the remaining dough balls. Cover each flattened ball with cling film and leave to rest for 15 minutes.
5. To make the filling, parboil the potatoes for 7 minutes. Allow to cool then carefully grate and set aside.

6. Using a food processor, blitz together the onion, garlic, red pepper, chilli, coriander and chives until a rough paste is formed.
7. In a small saucepan on a low heat, heat 1 teaspoon of oil and fry the paste for 30 seconds. Tip the paste into a large bowl and add the grated potato, grated cheeses, a pinch of salt and a grind of black pepper. Mix well.
8. Roll out each dough ball into a 25cm-diameter circle, then stack them up with a sheet of greaseproof paper between each.
9. Heat a large frying pan on a medium heat and brush the surface well with ghee. When the surface of the pan is hot, place a roti on to it then lower the heat right down. Cover the roti with one third of the filling, leaving a border clear around the edge, then take another roti and place it on top. Pinch tightly around the edges to seal them together. Brush the top of the roti with some ghee and cook for about 5 minutes, then carefully flip the roti over and cook for a further 5 minutes, until the roti and filling are cooked through. Make another two 'rotsties' in the same way.
10. Allow to cool for a couple minutes, slice into quarters and serve.

SOUPS & SALADS

Callaloo

SERVES 4-6

Callaloo is not only a wild form of spinach but also the name of this tasty dish which is made from it. Think of it as a thick, meaty, coconut-milk chowder with okra, leafy greens and a gorgeous blend of herbs. Callalloo leaves aren't a dime a dozen outside of the Caribbean, so humble (but nonetheless super) spinach is a great substitute. Along with okra, there is enough wholesome greenage here to satisfy even Popeye. If you wish, you can leave out the ham hock, and for something extra special, stir in a handful of cooked crabmeat or lobster meat before serving. Delish with Fried Bakes (see page 141).

TIME: 10 MINUTES PREP + 40 MINUTES COOKING

2 tbsp olive oil
1½ large onions, roughly chopped
3 large garlic cloves, crushed
5 fresh thyme sprigs
4½ tsp roughly chopped chives
3 tbsp roughly chopped flat-leaf parsley leaves
500g spinach, washed
175g okra, stems removed, roughly chopped
800ml coconut milk
600ml vegetable stock

1 small cooked ham hock, meat shredded and bone reserved
1 Scotch bonnet pepper, unpierced and unbruised
sea salt and freshly ground black pepper

1. Heat the oil in a large saucepan on a medium heat, then add the onion and a small pinch of salt and sauté until soft, stirring occasionally, for about 5 minutes.
2. Add the garlic and herbs and stir for about 30 seconds before adding the spinach, okra, coconut milk, stock, hock bone, a small handful of the ham hock and the Scotch bonnet.
3. Turn the heat up and bring to the boil, then reduce the heat, cover the pan and simmer for 30 minutes, stirring often, but very gently (so you don't burst the Scotch bonnet and release its fire!).
4. Remove the hock bone, the woody stalk of the thyme and the Scotch bonnet. Discard the first two but reserve the Scotch bonnet for later. Using a stick blender, blitz the Callaloo until it is smooth then stir through three-quarters of the shredded ham hock and season to taste. (You can prepare the recipe up to this stage and chill for a couple days, or freeze for up to 2 months and defrost before heating up.)
5. Serve in bowls, topping with the remaining shredded ham hock. For more heat, finely chop the reserved Scotch bonnet, discarding the seeds (or not, if you really want some fire), and sprinkle over the Callaloo.

Scallop, Puddin' & Sour

SERVES 4-6

Traditionally eaten at Christmas time, black pudding is so adored in the Caribbean that it has become an all-year-round treat! This recipe was inspired by the Guyanese, who often eat black pudding with a mango chutney called a sour. The sharp mango sour works beautifully with the black pudding and the sweet scallops, and a hint of Scotch bonnet adds some tropical pow to this simple salad.

TIME: 5 MINUTES PREP + 20 MINUTES COOKING

For the mango sour
1 large, ripe mango, peeled, stoned and roughly chopped
1 large garlic clove, crushed
⅛ Scotch bonnet pepper, seeded and finely chopped (use disposable gloves)
1 tsp white wine vinegar
juice of 1 lime
sea salt and freshly ground black pepper

For the salad
1½ tbsp olive oil
50g cubed pancetta
knob of butter
300g black pudding, cut into 10mm-thick slices

1½ tbsp extra virgin olive oil
250g rocket and spinach salad leaves, washed
24 scallops, shelled, trimmed, coral removed, cleaned and patted dry

1. To make the mango sour, pop all the ingredients into a small saucepan and cook on a high heat, stirring constantly, until the mango breaks down into a sort of purée, about 5 minutes.
2. Remove from the heat and stir in about 80–100ml water so that you have a thick salad-dressing consistency. Use a stick blender to blitz the sour until smooth, then season to taste and set aside. (You can prepare the recipe up to this stage and chill for up to 5 days.)
3. Heat the oil in a large frying pan on a medium heat and fry the pancetta until the fat has been rendered out and the pancetta is crisp and golden, about 2–3 minutes. Remove the pancetta with a slotted spoon and set aside for later.
4. Add a knob of butter to the same pan and melt on a medium-high heat. When the butter is frothy, add the black pudding and fry until crisp on the edges, black on both sides and cooked through, about 2–3 minutes per side. Remove the black pudding with a slotted spoon and keep warm.
5. To dress the leaves, whisk the olive oil with 2 tablespoons of the mango sour until mixed. Gently toss this dressing through the salad so that it coats the leaves and transfer to a serving dish.
6. Season the scallops. Remove any excess fat from the frying pan and place the pan on a high heat. Once it starts to

smoke, add the scallops and sear them for about a minute or so on each side until golden-brown and just cooked.
7. To serve, crumble the black pudding into the salad, gently toss through, then arrange the scallops on top, spooning a little more of the sour over them, and finally scatter over the pancetta. Serve immediately.

Carrot & Lentils

SERVES 6

This little gem of a salad is a perfectly quick, knock-up recipe for barbecues and picnics, as well as an ace accompaniment for cold cuts. I've worked familiar Caribbean spices into the other ingredients here to make this healthy, refreshing salad, which is packed with oodles of spiced savoury sweetness, tiny bursts of juicy raisin and crunchy cashew. If there is any left over, I like to stir through a large handful of cooked quinoa, or other grain, for a quick, tasty and wholesome lunch or dinner.

**TIME: 15 MINUTES PREP
+ 20 MINUTES COOKING**

150g puy lentils
500ml vegetable stock
4 large carrots, scrubbed and coarsely grated
120g raisins
40g cashew nuts, toasted and roughly chopped
¼ small red chilli, seeded and finely chopped
2 tsp finely chopped coriander leaves
½ tsp ground allspice
½ tsp ground cumin
¼ tsp grated fresh root ginger
2 tsp clear honey

**1 tbsp olive oil
sea salt and freshly ground black pepper**

1. Put the puy lentils into a medium saucepan with the stock (adding a little water, if necessary, so that the lentils are just submerged) and bring to the boil, then reduce the heat and gently simmer for about 20 minutes, until tender. Drain, then leave to cool to room temperature.
2. Mix the carrots, raisins, cashew nuts, chilli, coriander leaves, allspice, cumin and ginger into the lentils.
3. In a separate, small bowl, mix together the honey and the oil.
4. Just before serving, gently toss this dressing through the salad and season to taste.

Cauliflower & Coconut Soup with Lime & Garlic Croutons

SERVES 4-6

This is one of the simplest and most satisfying recipes around. Admittedly, pairing curry and cauliflower isn't really ground breaking, but the crunchy lime and garlic croutons atop this rich, spiced soup and the coconut-tanginess of the yoghurt really lift this dish to another level. And as it takes only 30 minutes to make, you can deliver a tasty, filling superstar of a home-made soup even at your most time-poor.

TIME: 10 MINUTES PREP + 20 MINUTES COOKING

3 tbsp virgin coconut oil
5 shallots, roughly chopped
3 celery sticks, roughly chopped
5 garlic cloves, crushed
3 tsp Madras curry powder
1½ tsp ground coriander
1½ tsp ground cumin
1.2 litres vegetable stock
1½ x 400ml cans coconut milk
1.5kg cauliflower florets, roughly chopped
4-6 tbsp Good coconut-milk yoghurt or thick Greek yoghurt
sea salt and freshly ground black pepper

For the croutons
1½ thick slices of bread, cut into 10mm cubes
1½ tbsp olive oil
⅓ tsp garlic granules
grated zest of 1 large lime

1. Pre-heat the oven to 200°C/Gas 6.
2. To make the soup, heat the coconut oil in a large pan on a medium heat. Add the shallots and celery and soften with a pinch of salt, for about 5 minutes, stirring occasionally.
3. Add the garlic, curry powder, ground coriander and cumin and stir for about 30 seconds, until the aroma from the garlic and spices is released, then add the stock, coconut milk and cauliflower. Bring the soup to the boil, then reduce the heat, pop the lid on and simmer, stirring occasionally, until the cauliflower is tender, about 20 minutes.
4. In the meantime, make the garlic croutons. Put the crouton ingredients plus a pinch of salt and pepper into a freezer bag, then seal the bag, shake it and turn it upside down to fully coat the cubes of bread in the oil and seasonings. Tip out on to a baking sheet and bake in the oven for about 5–6 minutes until crispy and golden. Remove from the oven and set aside to cool. (The croutons will last for up to a week in an airtight container.)
5. Use a stick blender to blitz the soup until smooth, then season to taste. (You can prepare the recipe up to this stage and chill for a couple days, or freeze for up to 2 months and defrost before heating through.)
6. Serve the soup in individual bowls, topped with a dollop of the yoghurt and scattered with the croutons.

Crab Backs

SERVES 4-8

This Caribbean version of a dressed crab – with added tropical flair, of course – is served warm. The Worcestershire sauce and Angostura bitters add an aromatic essence. You can make this in advance and chill until needed. Don't worry if the proportion of white to brown crabmeat isn't bang on, even 50/50 works here. Serve with doorstop slices of bread smothered in oodles of butter, or, for a healthier approach, a simple salad.

TIME: 10 MINUTES PREP + 10 MINUTES COOKING

45g butter
½ small onion, finely chopped
¼ yellow (or orange) pepper, seeded and diced
2 garlic cloves, crushed
¼ red chilli, stem removed, finely chopped
2 tbsp chopped chives
2 tbsp chopped parsley leaves
500g cooked white crabmeat
300g cooked brown crabmeat
8 tbsp breadcrumbs
1 tbsp Worcestershire sauce
½ tsp Angostura bitters
1 tsp fresh lime juice

sea salt and freshly ground black pepper
4–8 small crab shells, cleaned, for serving (optional)

1. Melt 25g of the butter in a frying pan on a low heat. Add the onion, pepper and a small pinch of salt, and soften for about 5 minutes, stirring often. Add the garlic, chilli, chives and parsley and cook, stirring continuously, for about 30 seconds. Set aside.
2. Pre-heat the grill to hot.
3. In a large bowl, gently fold (trying not to mush) together the crabmeat, breadcrumbs, Worcestershire sauce, Angostura bitters and lime juice until well incorporated.
4. Finally add the ingredients from the frying pan and gently fold through the crabmeat and breadcrumb mixture until well combined. Season to taste.
5. Divide the crab mixture between the crab shells, or shallow ramekins, and use the remaining 20g of butter to dot the top of the crab mixture. (You can prepare the recipe up to this stage in advance and refrigerate for 1 day.)
6. Place the filled crab backs under the grill until golden, about a couple of minutes. Serve immediately.

Ginger-Dressed Tomato, Orange & Red Onion Salad

SERVES 4–8

The addition of the ginger dressing and orange segments to this recipe provides a tropical twist to an otherwise straightforward classic, the tomato and red onion salad. As lovely as it is to bite into a juicy segment of unadulterated orange, dusting it with a little salt and drizzling it with this zesty ginger dressing enhances the 'orangeness' of the fruit. This is sublime alongside a charred steak and is a refreshing addition to a hot summer's day lunch.

TIME: 5–10 MINUTES PREP

4 small oranges
8 large vine tomatoes, stems removed, sliced into 5mm-thick slices
¼ red onion, finely sliced
sea salt and freshly ground black pepper

For the ginger–citrus dressing
60ml olive oil
30ml freshly squeezed orange juice
60ml freshly squeezed lime juice
3 tsp clear honey
3 tsp caster sugar
3 tsp grated fresh root ginger

1. To make the ginger–citrus dressing, whisk together all the ingredients, ensuring they are well combined. Season to taste and set aside.
2. To peel and remove the pith from the oranges, firstly roll the orange on a flat surface to 'loosen' the fruit. Cut both ends off the orange so that it can stand upright. Using a sharp knife, carefully cut away at the peel and the pith, following the curve of the orange as carefully as possible. Repeat with the remaining oranges and then segment.
3. Arrange the tomato, orange segments and red onion on a serving plate and pour over the dressing. Sprinkle over a pinch of sea salt and a grind of pepper.
4. Let it sit for 20 minutes at room temperature, to allow the flavours to develop and infuse, before serving.

Tamarind-Dressed Sweet Potato & Beetroot Salad

SERVES 4-6

This wholesome salad is a real treat for the taste buds, packed with the sweetness of the root vegetables, the crunchy saltiness of the chickpeas and the sourness from the tamarind. Tamarind is a tangy, pulpy, pod-like fruit that grows on trees. In the Caribbean, it is indispensable in balancing sauces, both sweet and savoury, and is also used in a lot of local confectionery (the tamarind ball is a particular weakness of mine). Although it sounds exotic, you are bound to have come across it, as it is a key ingredient in HP and Worcestershire sauces. You should be able to find the paste, or concentrate, in your local supermarket, possibly in the 'World' or 'Exotic' food aisle, and you may also come across the pods themselves in the fruit section. This salad is great served warm, but just as tasty at room temperature (and very picnic-friendly). Wear gloves, or wash your hands thoroughly after handling the beetroot, or it will stain you (and your clothing) red.

TIME: 10 MINUTES PREP + 1 HOUR COOKING

- 4 raw beetroot (around 600g), trimmed, peeled and cut into 10mm chunks
- 2 large sweet potatoes (around 600g), peeled and cut into 10mm chunks
- 100g rocket, washed

1 tbsp chopped fresh coriander
zest of ½ orange
sea salt and freshly ground black pepper

For the tamarind dressing
2 tbsp tamarind concentrate
60ml olive oil
juice of 1 orange
8 tsp clear honey
2 garlic cloves, crushed

For the crispy chickpeas
½ x 400g can chickpeas, drained and rinsed
1 tbsp olive oil
scant pinch of cayenne pepper

1. Pre-heat the oven to 200°C/Gas 6.
2. To make the tamarind dressing, whisk together the tamarind concentrate, oil, orange juice and honey, until combined. Add the garlic and season to taste.
3. In a large roasting tray, toss the beetroot with 8 tablespoons of the tamarind dressing. Pop the tray into the oven and bake for 15 minutes.
4. Remove the tin from the oven and add the sweet potato, along with 4 tablespoons of the tamarind dressing, tossing well to coat all the vegetables. Pop back into the oven and bake for another 35-50 minutes, giving the tray a shake every 15 minutes, until the beetroot and sweet potato are tender and cooked through.

5. In the meantime, place the chickpeas in another roasting tray and drizzle with the oil, ensuring that all are well coated. Sprinkle over the cayenne pepper, a pinch of salt and a grind of pepper. Pop into the oven and bake for 35–40 minutes, giving the tray a shake every 15 minutes, until the chickpeas are crispy.
6. Toss the rocket with a little of the remaining tamarind dressing, enough to lightly coat all the leaves. Add the sweet potato and beetroot and gently toss through. Season to taste, scatter over the crispy chickpeas, coriander and orange zest.

Corn Soup

SERVES 6–8

The street food scene in Trinidad has always been massive. Whether you're in the capital of Port-of-Spain, down on the beach by Maracas Bay or by the 'Doubles' vendors in the neighbourhood of Tacarigua, the food is as incredible today as it was when I was a child. When my pa did his nightly jog around the Savannah, my ma, sisters and I would wait around for him drinking coconut water from the nut, getting hungry from the appetising wafts coming from the vendors selling this corn soup. It is wholesome and simple (and low-cost) to make and is a meal in itself. If you want to make it more of a chowder, sprinkle over crispy bacon pieces before serving.

TIME: 5 MINUTES PREP + 50 MINUTES COOKING

40g butter
1 onion, roughly chopped
1 carrot, scrubbed and roughly chopped + ½ carrot, diced
1 celery stick, roughly chopped
60g yellow split peas
2 large garlic cloves, crushed
2 tbsp finely chopped chives
2 tbsp chopped curly-leaf parsley leaves
800ml vegetable stock
400ml milk

160g corn kernels (about 1 whole ear of corn)
2–3 whole ears of corn, cut in half (half an ear for each person)
¾ tsp cayenne pepper, plus a pinch to garnish
sea salt and freshly ground black pepper
1 tsp chopped curly-leaf parsley, to garnish

1. Melt the butter in a large saucepan on a medium heat. Add the onion, roughly chopped carrot and celery and a pinch of salt and soften for about 20 minutes, stirring occasionally.
2. In the meantime, to give the split peas a head start, pop them into a small pan of simmering water and allow to simmer on a low heat for 20 minutes. Drain and set aside.
3. Add the garlic, chives and parsley to the pan with the softened vegetables and stir for about 30 seconds, until the garlic aroma is released, then stir in the vegetable stock, milk, corn kernels and the drained split peas. Bring to the boil, then reduce the heat, cover with a lid and let the soup simmer for about 20 minutes, stirring occasionally, until the corn and split peas are tender and cooked through.
4. In the meantime, place the diced carrot in a medium saucepan of simmering water and simmer for about 10 minutes, then add the ears of corn and continue simmering for another 5 minutes or so, until the corn and the carrot are tender. Drain and set aside.
5. Use a stick blender to blitz the soup until smooth, then stir in the diced carrot and cayenne pepper and season to taste.

6. To serve, divide the soup between the soup bowls. Place a half ear of corn into each and top the corn with a knob of butter and a pinch of salt. Finally, scatter over the parsley and a pinch of cayenne pepper.

Roasted Coconut & Cucumber Salad

SERVES 6-8

The mellowness of the coconut adds a pleasant creaminess to this salad. Don't worry about the little sprinkling of Scotch bonnet, because the marvellous cooling properties of the cucumber balance (ish) this heat. Sometimes I add shredded, cooked chicken breast to make a light dinner or lunch. You could also chop the cucumber and coconut into really tiny pieces and serve as a salsa with tortilla chips to make a pleasant addition to the usual guacamole and tomato kinds.

TIME: 10 MINUTES PREP + 20 MINUTES COOKING

200g fresh coconut meat, in large pieces
2 tbsp finely chopped coriander leaves
2 garlic cloves, crushed
¼ Scotch bonnet pepper, seeded and finely chopped (use disposable gloves)
1 cucumber, peeled and sliced into long, 10mm-wide thin ribbons
sea salt and freshly ground black pepper

1. Pre-heat the oven to 160°C/Gas 3.
2. Pop the coconut on to a baking sheet and bake for about 20 minutes. Allow to cool then peel into thin ribbons.
3. In a large bowl, toss together all the ingredients, ensuring that everything is well mixed. Season to taste and serve.

Jerk Pulled Pork & Watermelon Salad

SERVES 6-8

A quintessential Jamaican classic, and one regularly featured in my childhood home, jerk needs no introduction and a jerk recipe simply could not be left out of this book! However, don't bring out the chicken wings to marinate just yet. I wanted to offer something that was a refreshing change to the norm, so here is a filling salad that packs all the jerk punch and complex spice layers that are so well loved, complemented by sweet and salted, lush watermelon and peppery watercress. This ultimate summer salad is a winner for picnics, barbecues and al-fresco lunches, and is divine piled into hot Fried Bakes (see page 141) or crusty rolls.

TIME: 10 MINUTES PREP + 7 HOURS COOKING

2.5kg pork shoulder, bone in, skin removed, flesh deeply scored
100g watercress
¼ large watermelon, cut into small, bite-sized pieces
sea salt and freshly ground black pepper

For the marinade/dressing
1 portion Jerk Marinade (see page 273)
½ tbsp instant coffee granules, dissolved in 1 tbsp hot water
juice of 2 oranges

1. Pre-heat the oven to 220°C/Gas 7.
2. Combine half the Jerk Marinade with the dissolved coffee and half of the orange juice. Place the pork shoulder on to a plate and massage the jerk mixture deep into the scored flesh. Transfer the pork (leaving behind but not discarding, any excess juices on the plate) into a roasting tin and pop into the oven, uncovered, for 30 minutes.
3. Remove the tin from the oven and reduce the temperature to 150°C/Gas 2. Pour the excess juices from the plate over the pork shoulder, cover the tin with foil, ensuring that the edges are well sealed, and place back into the oven. Cook for 5–7 hours, turning the shoulder and spooning the tray juices over every hour, until the meat is cooked through and can be literally spooned off the bone. Remove the pork shoulder from the oven and set aside, loosely covered with the foil.
4. In the meantime, on a low heat, heat the remaining marinade in a small saucepan for a couple of minutes, stirring occasionally, until the spice aroma hits you, then stir in the remaining orange juice to make a dressing. Set aside 2 tablespoons of this dressing for later.
5. When the pork shoulder is cool enough to handle, remove and discard any fat, then use a fork to pull the meat from the bone and place in a large bowl, along with any sticky

juices left in the tin. Using two forks, shred the meat into bite-sized pieces.

6. Pour the dressing over the pulled pork, gently tossing to ensure that it is well coated in the liquid. Taste and adjust the seasoning, if necessary. (Once the pork has cooled to room temperature, you can chill it for a couple days, or freeze for up to 2 months and defrost fully, before heating through.)

7. In the meantime, put the watercress on a large serving platter and pour over the reserved 2 tablespoons of dressing, ensuring that all the leaves are well coated. Add the watermelon and a generous pinch of salt (it needs a lot!), tossing it through to ensure that the watermelon is well seasoned. Add the pulled pork and gently toss together, distributing the shreds of pork across the salad. Have a final taste, and add a little more seasoning, if necessary, before serving.

For the barbecue

Marinate the shoulder with the jerk marinade, coffee and orange juice mixture overnight. Soak a couple of handfuls of wood chips (maple, apple or oak are best) in cold water for about an hour, then drain. Pre-heat the barbecue to a very low heat (between 100°C and 150°C), pushing all the coals to one side of the barbecue. Pop the wood chips on top of the coals. On the opposite side, place an aluminium tray and fill it halfway with water (keep topping up as the water evaporates). Place the grate on and pop the prepared pork shoulder on to the grate above the aluminium tray and cover the barbecue with the lid. Cook for about 5-7 hours, until the internal temperature of the pork reaches 90°C. If the shoulder isn't quite dark and crispy enough, whack the heat up on the barbecue and cook for a few minutes until that burnished look is achieved. Carefully remove the shoulder from the grate (it will almost be falling apart) and allow it to rest for 30 minutes, loosely covered with foil. Serve as above.

(You can also start the pork shoulder on the barbecue and after a couple of hours finish the cooking in the oven.)

Zaboca Gazpacho

SERVES 6

Gazpachos are particularly personal, so make it as thick or as watery as you like, just make sure you have it chilled. You can really have fun with different toppings, too: sometimes, I garnish it with some cubed feta cheese and croutons, or even, if I'm feeling extravagant, with cooked crab or lobster meat. Make it in bulk and store in the fridge for a few days.

TIME: 10 MINUTES PREP + 2 HOURS CHILLING

2½ large, ripe avocados
2 large cucumbers, peeled, seeded and roughly chopped
2 large garlic cloves, crushed
½ red onion, roughly chopped
1 tbsp roughly chopped chives
1 tsp roughly chopped coriander leaves + 1 tsp finely chopped coriander leaves
250ml vegetable stock, at room temperature
juice of 1 lime
2 tbsp sherry vinegar
2 tbsp extra virgin olive oil, plus extra to drizzle
1 tsp paprika, plus a pinch to garnish
2 tsp caster sugar

sea salt and freshly ground black pepper
1 tsp finely chopped mint leaves, to garnish

1. Peel, stone and roughly chop two of the avocados and, in a large bowl, using a stick blender, blitz together with the cucumber, garlic, red onion, chives and 1 teaspoon of the coriander until you have a smooth purée.
2. Stir in the vegetable stock, lime juice, sherry vinegar, olive oil and paprika. Add about 80–100ml water, depending on how thick you like your gazpacho. Season to taste with the sugar, salt and black pepper. Pop in the fridge for a couple of hours, until chilled.
3. To serve, chop the flesh of the remaining avocado into small cubes. Divide the gazpacho between bowls, top with the avocado cubes, drizzle over some olive oil, scatter over the mint and finely chopped coriander leaves and sprinkle with a small pinch of paprika.

Green Mango & Sour Apple Chow

SERVES 4–6

Chow is any fruit, or sometimes veg, that has been chopped into bite-sized pieces and usually seasoned with garlic, chilli, shado beni (a wild form of coriander) and salt. The result is a quick and simple, moreish, light snacking salad, perfect for enjoying on a hot day with an ice-cold beer, or served up with the barbecue spread – ideally at the beach! Most supermarkets sell half-ripe mangoes for ripening up at home and these are perfect for this recipe. Bramley apple has a sourness that makes it a bang-on substitute for the Caribbean fruit, pomme cythere (also known as june plum or golden apple). This is one of my favourite things. My mouth waters just thinking about it.

TIME: 15 MINUTES PREP + 15 MINUTES 'DEVELOPING'

- 1 large, unripe, firm mango, peeled, stoned and chopped into small bite-sized chunks
- 1 large Bramley apple, cored, and chopped into small bite- sized chunks
- sea salt and freshly ground black pepper

For the dressing
1½ tbsp olive oil
1 tbsp lime juice
½ tsp Pepper Sauce (see page 258)

2 large garlic cloves, crushed
1 tbsp finely chopped coriander leaves
1 tbsp white wine vinegar

1. In a bowl, whisk together the dressing ingredients and season to taste.
2. Add the mango and apple and leave to sit and soak in the flavour for 15 minutes before eating. Keep for up to 2 days in the fridge.

Blackened Corn Salad

SERVES 4-6

There are many reasons to love this salad: it is so flavoursome, so good for you and so simple to make! It is a perfect side salad to accompany simple grilled or barbecued meats and fish. Don't be tempted to buy tinned sweetcorn, though, because the chargrilled flavour that comes from griddling or barbecuing the corn is what really gives this salad its ping. For something a little more filling, just stir in a portion of cooked rice.

TIME: 5 MINUTES PREP + 12 MINUTES COOKING

4 ears of corn
1½ tbsp olive oil, plus extra for coating the corn
4 spring onions
1 red pepper, seeded and finely diced
100g cored fresh pineapple, cut into 1cm chunks
1 tsp lime juice
pinch of cayenne pepper
2 tsp finely chopped coriander leaves
2 tsp finely chopped chives
1 tsp finely chopped flatleaf parsley
sea salt and freshly ground black pepper

1. Heat a griddle pan on a high heat.
2. Coat the ears of corn with a little oil and sprinkle with a little salt and pepper. When the griddle pan is smoking hot, pop the corn on and cook for about 7 minutes, turning regularly, until blistered and evenly charred all over.
3. Place the charred corn into a bowl and cover with cling film for about 5 minutes, to steam from the residual heat, until tender.
4. In the meantime, place the spring onions on to the hot griddle pan for about 2–3 minutes, turning halfway, until lightly charred.
5. Finely chop the charred spring onions and pop them into a large bowl along with the diced red pepper and the pineapple chunks.
6. Standing the corn ears on their ends, use a knife to carefully slice down the ears to carve away the kernels. Add the kernels to the bowl of spring onions and diced pepper. Separate any connected kernels, then add the oil, lime juice, cayenne pepper and herbs and mix well. Season to taste, give a final stir and serve immediately.

For the barbecue
Pre-heat the barbecue until the coals have just turned white. Pop the prepared ears of corn on to the grate over the hottest part of the barbecue and cook for 2–3 minutes on each side, basting often with oil (to ensure that they don't dry out), until the kernels are lightly charred and tender. Brush the spring onion with a little oil and pop on to the grate over the hottest part of the barbecue for a few minutes turning halfway through, until lightly charred all over. Serve as above.

Mock Conch Salad

SERVES 4-6

This is a tropical ceviche recipe, inspired by the Bahamian conch version and something of a must-have snack for the beach. I have used sea bass instead of the traditional sea snail, and it works really well. The acid in the citrus 'cooks' the protein in the fish. And you need only glance at the remaining ingredients to see all the flavour that is imparted into this light delight of a dish.

TIME: 5 MINUTES PREP + 2 HOURS CHILLING

- ½ pink (or red) grapefruit
- 3 sushi-grade sea bass fillets (about 500g), skinned and cut into 0.5-1cm cubes
- juice of 2 large oranges
- juice of 1 large lime
- ½ yellow pepper, stem removed, seeded and finely diced into roughly 1cm cubes
- ½ small red onion, finely chopped
- 1 small, firm tomato, stem removed, seeded and finely diced
- 1 tsp finely chopped coriander leaves
- ¼-½ tsp finely chopped Scotch bonnet pepper (use disposable gloves)
- 1 tbsp extra virgin olive oil
- 1 tsp caster sugar
- sea salt and freshly ground black pepper

1. Peel and remove the pith from the grapefruit. First roll the grapefruit on a flat surface to loosen the fruit. Cut both ends off the grapefruit so that it can stand upright. Using a sharp knife, carefully cut away at the peel and the pith, following the curve of the grapefruit as carefully as possible. Separate into segments and cut into 1cm cubes.
2. Place the sea bass fillet cubes into a small bowl. In a separate bowl, gently mix together the citrus juices, grapefruit, pepper, onion, tomato, coriander, Scotch bonnet, olive oil and sugar and season to taste with salt and pepper.
3. Pour the mixture over the sea bass so that it is immersed (or almost immersed), cover tightly with cling film (the cling film should actually touch the surface of the salad) and pop into the fridge to chill for 2 hours. If any of the sea bass isn't covered by the citrus juices, gently toss the ingredients halfway through the chilling time so that any 'uncovered' sea bass on the top is now covered.
4. To serve, pile the sea bass, along with the accompanying fruit and vegetables, into a shallow serving bowl. Drizzle over the marinating juice and sprinkle with a pinch of salt (this dish can really take the salt). Serve immediately.

ONE POT

ONE POT

Pelau

SERVES 8–10

Visiting Sangre Grande in Trinidad usually means spending time with my maternal Mama and chowing down on Aunty Verna's delicious pelau. Pelau is a rice-based dish, usually with chicken and salty pig-tail (yup! I've used ham-hock to give a similar salty tone), that would be cooked early in the morning to take down to the beach to enjoy between bouts of sea bathing. This ultimate one-pot dish tastes delicious with a good splosh of Pepper Sauce (see page 258) and is even more scrumptious a day later and at room temperature. If you want to make this veggie, just add the Green Seasoning (see page 271) with the gungo peas and stir through cooked butternut squash, sweetcorn and any other veg just before the rice has finished cooking.

TIME: 10 MINUTES PREP + OVERNIGHT MARINATING + 35 MINUTES COOKING

1.6kg skinless, boneless chicken thighs and breasts, chopped into 2.5cm chunks
5 tbsp Green Seasoning (see page 271)
½ thumb-sized piece of fresh root ginger, peeled and grated
1 large garlic clove, crushed
5 tbsp olive oil
4 tbsp demerara sugar

½ small cooked ham hock, shredded, fat discarded
500g long-grain rice, rinsed thoroughly
1.2 litres chicken stock
50g coconut cream, grated
1 large whole Scotch bonnet pepper, unpierced and unbruised
2 x 400g cans gungo peas, drained and rinsed
2 large red peppers, seeded and finely chopped
1 carrot, scrubbed and finely chopped into 1cm cubes
couple of splashes of soy sauce
splash of Angostura bitters
sea salt and freshly ground black pepper
1 tbsp finely chopped chives, to garnish

1. Place the chicken in a bowl with the Green Seasoning, ginger, garlic and 1 tablespoon of the oil. Mix well, cover and leave to marinate in the fridge overnight.
2. The next day, heat 1 tablespoon of the oil in a large, heavy-based casserole dish on a medium–hot heat until it starts to smoke. Add the demerara sugar and stir continuously until it dissolves and starts turning very dark brown and frothy, about 1–2 minutes. Immediately, add the chicken pieces, stirring continuously to brown the meat well in the caramel then, using a slotted spoon, remove the chicken pieces and set aside for later.
3. Heat another tablespoon of oil then stir in the ham hock and the rice, making sure that you coat the grains in the oil. Add the stock, creamed coconut and Scotch bonnet and bring to the boil. As soon as the liquid starts to boil, pop the lid on so it only partially covers the pot and

continue boiling until the liquid has been reduced enough so that the rice is just peeking up from the surface of the water.

4. Reduce the heat to a simmer and add the browned chicken, gungo peas, red pepper and carrot and cook for a couple of minutes. Add the remaining 2 tablespoons of oil and gently stir through (trying not to pierce the Scotch bonnet) so that it coats the rice well. Continue cooking on a low heat, with the lid on, until the chicken is cooked through, any remaining liquid has evaporated and the rice is just tender, about 20–25 minutes.

5. Carefully remove the Scotch bonnet. Use a fork to gently fluff the rice and mix in the soy sauce and the Angostura bitters. Season to taste. Chop in a fingernail-sized piece of the cooked Scotch bonnet if you fancy a little extra heat. Top with the chives and serve immediately or leave to cool to room temperature to take to the beach!

Curried Duck

SERVES 6–8

Here is a mouthwatering, national-status dish, hailing from Trinidad. This is the perfect dish for 'liming' (see page 13) down by the river, where friends and randoms gather, with ice cold Caribs in hand, to dig into a sharing pot of curry. Obviously, there is Indian inspiration and derivation behind this dish, but a Caribbean curry is really so distinct that you simply must try it to 'get' it. If you don't fancy meat, leave out the duck and instead marinate a mixture of root vegetables. I strongly recommend that you serve this in the traditional fashion, with Buss-Up Shut (see page 149), but if you are really strapped for time, then a little cooked rice will do, I suppose . . .

TIME: OVERNIGHT MARINATING + 10 MINUTES PREP + 1 HOUR 10 MINUTES COOKING

- 1 large duck, or 3kg mixed duck breast and legs, skinned, breast meat cut into bite-sized chunks and legs kept whole
- 3 tbsp olive oil, plus an extra drizzle
- 1 large onion, finely chopped
- 3 tbsp amchar masala (see page 279)
- 8 tbsp Madras curry powder
- 12 new potatoes, peeled and cut into 2.5cm cubes
- 2 x 400g cans chickpeas, drained and rinsed

sea salt and freshly ground black pepper
Buss-Up Shut (see page 149), to serve (optional)

For the marinade
4½ tbsp roughly chopped coriander leaves
3 tbsp roughly chopped chives
1½ tbsp roughly chopped thyme leaves
6 garlic cloves, crushed
¾ thumb-sized piece of ginger, peeled and grated
¾ Scotch bonnet pepper, seeded and roughly chopped (use gloves)
2 tbsp good-quality dark rum
2 tbsp olive oil

1. Pop all the marinade ingredients into a food processor, along with a generous pinch of salt, and blitz until a smooth paste is formed.
2. Place the duck pieces in a large freezer bag and add the marinade. Squeezing out the air and leaving space for the duck to move in the bag, seal the bag and then massage the marinade deep into the duck, ensuring that all the pieces are well coated. Leave in the fridge to marinate overnight.
3. The following day, heat the oil in a large casserole or saucepan on a medium heat. Add the onion and soften, with a little salt, stirring regularly, for about 5–10 minutes.
4. Add the amchar masala and curry powder and stir for about a minute, until there is no dry powder remaining and the spice aromas hit you. Add about 200ml water and cook until the liquid thickens into a paste, about 2–5 minutes.

5. Add a little drizzle of oil, then the duck and cook for about 10–15 minutes, until browned all over, stirring regularly.
6. Pour in 750ml water, bring to the boil, then add the potato, reduce the heat to low, cover the pan and simmer for about 30 minutes, stirring occasionally, until thickened.
7. Finally, add the chickpeas and cook for a further 10 minutes, until the duck is cooked through. Crush a few of the potatoes into the sauce to thicken the curry a little. Season to taste and serve with a folded tea towel full of Buss-Up Shut.

Geera Pork Chops with Citrus Garlic Gremolata

SERVES 6

Geera, or cumin pork, is an extremely popular 'cutter' (nibble to have with drinks) and is usually made simply with small cubes of pork, a touch of seasoning and of course, cumin. Now and again, when just a little nibble won't quite 'cut' it, I like to amp it up into a full-blown pork-chop dinner. The cumin still sings out, but the pleasant addition of vegetables and a zesty gremolata add another layer of flavour and texture. It is showy enough to serve at a dinner party, but also quick and wholesome enough for a mid-week meal, as you just bung the whole thing in the oven and you can prepare the gremolata in advance. A lovely British–Caribbean fusion dish!

TIME: 20 MINUTES PREP + OVERNIGHT MARINATING + 50 MINUTES COOKING

6 thick pork chops, on the bone
300g butternut squash, peeled and cut into 2cm cubes, parboiled for 5 minutes
2 large red onions, cut into eighths
2 large yellow peppers, seeded and cut into large pieces
2 carrots, scrubbed, sliced lengthways down the centre and into 5cm spears
3 tomatoes, quartered
1 garlic bulb, unpeeled, cloves separated and smashed

2 tbsp olive oil (or a large knob of butter), plus extra oil to drizzle
sea salt and freshly ground black pepper

For the marinade
3 tbsp Green Seasoning (see page 271)
⅛ Scotch bonnet pepper, seeded and finely chopped
3 garlic cloves, crushed
1 tbsp olive oil

For the spice rub
1½ tbsp cumin seeds, crushed
½ tsp ground fenugreek
½ tsp ground fennel
½ tsp ground black peppercorns
½ tsp brown mustard seeds, crushed
½ tsp ground coriander

For the gremolata
grated zest of 1 lemon
grated zest of 1 lime
1 garlic clove, crushed
1 tbsp finely chopped flat-leaf parsley leaves
1 tbsp finely chopped coriander leaves

1. Combine all the marinade ingredients in a large bowl. Add the pork chops, coating them well, then cover the bowl with cling film and leave to marinate in the fridge overnight.

2. The next day, combine all the spice rub ingredients in a small bowl. Wipe away any excess marinade from the pork chops and rub the dry spices into the meat, coating both sides well. Sprinkle with a little salt and pepper. Set aside at room temperature for 30 minutes to 1 hour.
3. Pre-heat the oven to 175°C/Gas 4.
4. Pop the vegetables and garlic in a large roasting tin, drizzle with a little olive oil and sprinkle with a little salt and pepper and pop into the oven for 25 minutes, then set aside.
5. Heat the oil (or butter) in a large frying pan on a medium heat, then pop the chops in and sear for a couple minutes on each side, until they start to brown and crisp up on the outside. Place the seared chops on top of the vegetables in the roasting tin.
6. Pour any remaining fat in the frying pan over the pork chops, tent the pan loosely with foil, tightly seal the edges and pop into the oven for about 10-15 minutes, until the chops are just cooked through (the juices should run clear when the pork is pierced). Let rest with the foil still covering, for a few minutes.
7. To make the gremolata, mix together all the ingredients in a bowl using a fork.
8. Transfer the pork chops and veg to a large serving platter so that everyone can help themselves. Pour the juices into a little jug so that it can be drizzled over the chops as desired. Serve with the gremolata, to scatter over.

For the barbecue

Pre-heat the barbecue until the coals have just turned white. Make two large foil 'envelopes' and place half the vegetables into each one, then add the oil and a splash of water to each before sealing the envelopes tightly (but leaving space inside the envelope). Place the vegetable envelopes on to the barbecue and cook for about 30 minutes, turning occasionally, until the vegetables are cooked through and tender. For the pork, pop the prepared chops on to the grate over the hottest part of the barbecue and sear for a couple minutes on each side, until they start to brown and crisp a little. Move the chops to the coolest part of the barbecue and continue to cook for about 4 minutes on each side, with the barbecue lid down, until just cooked through. Allow to rest before serving with the vegetables, the vegetable juices and the gremolata, as above.

Curried Crab & Dumplings

SERVES 4-6

A perfect example of the versatility of Caribbean food: though based on a Tobagonian beach snack, this dish also makes a pretty amazing winter warmer. You will definitely want to have Fried Bakes (see page 141) or doorstop wedges of bread to hand for mopping up the sauce. It is usually made with whole crab, but I think crab claws offer enough opportunity to adopt the Caribbean hands-on approach to eating without turning the meal into a completely sloppy farce! (There is a reason that this dish is eaten on the beach: that way you jump straight into the sea afterwards to wash it all off!)

TIME: 5 MINUTES PREP + 35 MINUTES COOKING

- 3 tbsp olive oil
- 1½ large onions, finely chopped
- 4 garlic cloves, crushed
- 6 tsp finely chopped chives
- 2 tsp finely chopped flat-leaf parsley leaves plus 1 tsp to garnish
- 2 tsp finely chopped thyme leaves plus ½ tsp finely chopped leaves, to garnish
- thumb-sized piece of fresh root ginger, peeled and grated
- 3 tsp ground cumin
- 3 tsp ground turmeric

4 tbsp amchar masala (see page 279)
5 large tomatoes, roughly chopped into 1cm chunks
1 x 400ml can coconut milk
1 Scotch bonnet pepper, unpierced and unbruised
100g cooked mixed crabmeat
12 cooked crab claws
1 lime, cut into 6 wedges
sea salt and freshly ground black pepper

For the polenta dumplings
170g self-raising flour, sifted
170g polenta
1½ tsp baking powder
200ml milk

1. Heat the oil in a large saucepan on a medium heat. Add the onion and a small pinch of salt and soften, stirring often, for about 5 minutes.
2. Add the garlic, herbs, ginger and spices and stir for a minute, then add the tomato and coconut milk and increase the heat to bring to the boil. When the liquid begins to boil, turn the heat right down to a gentle simmer, add the Scotch bonnet and continue to simmer for 15 minutes, stirring occasionally, but gently so that you don't burst the Scotch bonnet skin and release the heat! (You can prepare the recipe up to this stage and refrigerate for up to 2 days in advance.)
3. In the meantime, pop the dry dumpling ingredients into a small bowl, along with a pinch of salt, and use a fork to mix thoroughly. Gradually add the milk (you may not need to

use it all) and stir until the mixture comes together to form a dough.
4. Tip the dough out on to a lightly floured surface and knead for a couple of minutes.
5. Roll the dough into a long sausage shape about 4cm in diameter. Slice into 1cm-thick discs then flatten each with the palm of your hand and add these to the curry. Pop the lid on to the pan and leave until the dumplings are cooked, about 10 minutes, adding the crabmeat and claws after 5 minutes. Season to taste.
6. To serve, empty the curry into serving bowls, scatter over the remaining parsley and thyme and top with the lime wedges.

Red Bean & Spinach Mac 'n' Cheese

SERVES 6-8

My little sis, Ash, is obsessed with this dish, which is familiar in a way but with an added zing that hints of jerk seasoning. If you want to make this a full-blown jerk mac just add a few teaspoons of my Jerk Marinade (see page 273). A big reason for including it here is that it is a loving nod to a dish I was brought up on: macaroni pie. Admittedly this is more supple and wet compared to the stalwart macaroni pie, which stands upright like a slice of cake, but it's still to die for.

TIME: 10 MINUTES PREP + 30 MINUTES COOKING

500g macaroni
50g unsalted butter
2 tbsp plain flour
3 spring onions, bulb removed, finely chopped
7 garlic cloves, crushed
5 bay leaves
1 litre milk
200g mature Cheddar, grated
105g Parmesan, grated
1 tsp chopped thyme leaves
1 tsp ground allspice
1 tsp paprika
½ tsp cayenne pepper

4 tbsp Molasses and Rum Barbecue Sauce (see page 260, or other rich, smoky barbecue sauce)
200g spinach, washed
1 x 400g can kidney beans, drained and rinsed
6 tbsp breadcrumbs
sea salt and freshly ground black pepper

1. Pre-heat the grill to hot.
2. Cook the macaroni in a large saucepan of salted, boiling water according to the instructions on the packet, until tender. Drain and set aside.
3. Meanwhile, make a roux by melting 35g of the butter in a large pan on a low heat, add the flour and whisk continuously. Increase the heat to medium until you have a paste. Add the spring onions, garlic and bay leaves and whisk continuously for a couple of minutes. Gradually whisk in the milk, a little at a time, until smooth. Bring to the boil, then reduce to a simmer, whisking occasionally, until thickened and smooth, about 10 to 15 minutes.
4. Stir in the Cheddar and 75g of the Parmesan, along with the thyme and spices, the Barbecue Sauce and finally the spinach, kidney beans and drained pasta. Stir until well combined, season to taste then tip into a large, wide, heatproof casserole dish.
5. Melt the remaining 15g of butter in a small pan on a low heat and mix in the breadcrumbs and remaining 35g of Parmesan. Spread this evenly over the top of the Mac 'n' Cheese and pop the whole dish under the grill for about 5 minutes until bubbling and golden-brown. Serve immediately.

Lamb Pepperpot

SERVES 4-6

Pepperpot is one of the quintessential one-pot Caribbean dishes. Originally from Guyana, the dish has spread throughout the Caribbean islands, each country adding its own individual flair and take on the dish. Traditionally, it was made with any available meat or fish, and usually included pig's tail or trotters or cow heel. A key ingredient is 'cassareep': a thick, molasses-like liquid from the root of bitter cassava (highly poisonous if not cooked properly). Originally added as a preservative, it is now key to the flavour of the dish. It's difficult to find cassareep outside of the Caribbean, so instead I've used molasses sugar, white wine vinegar and lime to create a similar flavour. Authentic pepperpot wouldn't normally contain the vegetables I have included but, as is the Caribbean way, once you have acknowledged the key flavour of the dish, you can go ahead and add whatever you have lying around the kitchen. I have taken some inspiration from Lancashire lamb hotpot and layered slices of potato on top for a crispy element. You can make this into a veggie's delight by leaving out the lamb and including lots of veg (butternut squash, peas, carrots, whatever's around at the time). Wholesome and hearty, this one pot is a winner!

TIME: 15 MINUTES PREP + 2 ¾ HOURS COOKING

50ml olive oil, plus a little extra for brushing
60g butter

1kg stewing lamb, cut into in 2.5cm chunks
2 onions, finely chopped
4 garlic cloves, crushed
¼ cinnamon stick
6 cloves
1 tbsp finely chopped thyme leaves
½ tbsp finely chopped chives
3 bay leaves
20g plain flour
pared zest of ¼ orange
500ml vegetable stock
4 tbsp tomato purée
2 tsp Worcestershire sauce
1 tsp Angostura Bitters
4 tbsp white wine vinegar
2 tbsp lime juice
2 tbsp molasses sugar
1 Scotch bonnet pepper, unpierced and unbruised
300g aubergine, skin on, stem removed, cut into 2.5cm cubes
400g new potatoes, skin on, cut into 5mm slices
sea salt and freshly ground black pepper

1. Pre-heat the oven to 150°C/Gas 2.
2. Heat the oil and 35g of butter in a large casserole pan on a very high heat. Add the diced lamb and brown in batches. Set aside on a plate for later.
3. Reduce the heat to medium, heat 15g of butter and soften the onion with a little salt, stirring often, for about 5 minutes. Add the garlic, cinnamon, cloves and herbs and

cook for 30 seconds, stirring constantly, until the aroma is released.

4. Stir in the flour, then the orange zest, stock, tomato purée, Worcestershire sauce, Angostura bitters, vinegar, lime juice, sugar and Scotch bonnet. Bring to the boil then reduce to a low simmer. Add the lamb and simmer with the lid off, stirring often, until thick, about 20–30 minutes. Remove from the heat.

5. Remove the cinnamon stick, orange peel, bay leaves and Scotch bonnet. Stir in the aubergine and layer the potato slices, overlapping them, on the top of the Pepperpot. Brush the potato with a little oil, cover the casserole with a lid and bake in the oven for 2 hours. (You can prepare the recipe up to this stage, allow to cool and chill in the fridge for up to 2 days, or freeze for up to 2 months, defrosting fully before the final step.)

6. Remove the lid from the casserole and dot the potato with the remaining 10g of butter. Place under a medium-high grill for about 5 minutes, until the potato is golden brown. Serve immediately.

Salt Beef Oil Down

SERVES 6–8

The national dish of Grenada is so simple to make and is an exotic, one-of-a-kind type of stew. It is traditionally made with breadfruit (a fruit that, when cooked, tastes like, wait for it . . . bread) but I like the substitute my Ma would use: green, unripe bananas. The salt beef combines deliciously with the sweet coconut and spices, but salted pork (ham hock) also does the trick. Even though this is perfect eaten in a hot climate, it's also great when it's cold and miserable outside. To make this recipe even easier, you can use a ready-cooked salt beef joint, or, for a quick veggie fix, substitute the beef for some root vegetables, adding them at the same time as the green banana.

TIME: 10 MINUTES PREP + 3 HOURS

1kg uncooked salt beef joint
2 tbsp olive oil
1 large onion, finely chopped
1 celery stick, finely chopped
2 garlic cloves, crushed
1 tbsp finely chopped chives
1 tbsp finely chopped thyme leaves
1 tsp ground turmeric
2 x 400ml cans coconut milk
200g spinach

6 unripe, firm, green bananas, peeled and cut into 4cm-long slices
1 Scotch bonnet pepper, unpierced and unbruised
sea salt and freshly ground black pepper

1. Pop the beef joint into a large saucepan, cover fully with cold water and bring very gently to simmering point. Skim off any surface scum, then reduce the heat to the lowest setting and continue to gently poach, with the lid on, for about 2–2½ hours, ensuring that the joint is always covered with water and skimming off any surface scum, until a knife easily slides into the joint and it is cooked through. Remove the beef from the water and set aside.
2. Empty the water from the pan, add the oil and place on a medium heat, then add the onion and celery and soften with a pinch of salt, stirring often, for about 5 minutes.
3. Add the garlic, herbs and turmeric and stir for 30 seconds, until the aromas are released. Add the coconut milk, spinach, green banana and Scotch bonnet and bring to the boil, then reduce to a simmer for 20 minutes, stirring occasionally (but gently so that you don't burst the Scotch bonnet). Remove the Scotch bonnet.
4. Chop the salt beef joint into 2.5cm chunks, add to the pot and continue to simmer gently, until the liquid has evaporated away and you are left with a thick gravy and the banana is tender and cooked through, about 15–30 minutes. Season to taste and serve immediately.

Coconut Chicken 'Rundown'

SERVES 4-6

'Rundown' refers to the reducing down of coconut milk and so it follows, within Caribbean logic, that anything cooked in coconut milk becomes a rundown! One of the things I love about it is the way that the coconut-poached pumpkin literally melts away in your mouth with a subtle spiced sweetness. You can, of course, add any other veg and leave out the chicken, or indeed use a meaty fish instead; it will work just as well. Have some Fried Bakes (see page 141) on hand to mop up the lush sauce.

TIME: 15 MINUTES PREP + 45 MINUTES COOKING

½ thumb-sized piece of fresh root ginger, peeled and grated
4 garlic cloves, crushed
½ chilli, stem removed, seeded and roughly chopped
3 tbsp olive oil
1 onion, finely chopped
½ tbsp finely chopped thyme leaves
3 tbsp amchar masala (see page 279)
3 black peppercorns, crushed
5 allspice berries, crushed
½ tbsp chilli powder
½ tbsp ground turmeric

1 x 400ml can coconut milk
400g butternut squash, peeled, seeded and cut into 3cm cubes
900g skinless and boneless chicken pieces (thigh or breast, or a mixture), cut into 3cm cubes
sea salt and freshly ground black pepper

1. Using a mortar and pestle, bash together the ginger, garlic and chilli with a pinch of salt until you have a rough paste.
2. Heat the oil in a large saucepan on a low heat and soften the onions with a little salt, stirring often, for about 5 minutes.
3. Add the thyme, the ginger and garlic paste and the spices and cook for about 30 seconds, stirring constantly until the aroma is released. Add the coconut milk and butternut squash and bring to the boil, then reduce the heat and simmer, uncovered, for about 20 minutes.
4. Add the chicken and continue to simmer on a low heat, covered, until the chicken is cooked through, about 10 minutes, then simmer, with the lid off, until the pumpkin is tender and the sauce has thickened, another 5-10 minutes. Season to taste and serve.

Shellfish Chowder

SERVES 4-6

Originating from the Bahamas, this is a non-cream-based chowder that would usually be made with conch. A light, but fully satisfying one-pot meal brimming with a spiced, 'herby' flavour that really enhances the natural sweet-saltiness of the mussels, clams and cockles (a fantastic substitute for the conch). I usually serve it with a little side salad – or wedges of soft bread, drizzled with olive oil, to soak up the tasty shellfish broth – and definitely with some Pepper Sauce (see page 258) to hand.

TIME: 15 MINUTES PREP + 45 MINUTES COOKING

- 700g mixed mussels, clams and cockles, washed and scrubbed
- 3 tbsp olive oil
- 80g bacon lardons
- 1 large onion, finely chopped
- 1 celery stick, finely chopped
- 1 green pepper, seeded and cut into 1cm cubes
- 1 carrot, scrubbed and finely diced into 5mm cubes
- 3 garlic cloves, crushed
- 2 bay leaves
- 1 tbsp dried oregano
- ½ tbsp finely chopped thyme leaves

½ tbsp dried marjoram
½ tsp cayenne pepper
2 x 400g cans chopped plum tomatoes
2 tbsp tomato purée
800ml fish stock
1 tbsp sherry vinegar
1 tsp Pepper Sauce (see page 258)
4 new potatoes, peeled and diced into 1cm cubes
300g raw prawns
sea salt and freshly ground black pepper
crusty bread, to serve

1. Place the mussels, clams and cockles in a large saucepan with a little water, pop the lid on and cook on a high heat for a few minutes until the shells open.
2. Remove from the heat and drain the shellfish into a colander, reserving the cooking liquor for later. When cool enough to handle, remove the meat from the shells and set aside for later.
3. Heat a little of the oil in a large pan on a medium heat and fry the bacon, onion, celery, pepper and carrot with a little salt, stirring often, for about 10 minutes, until soft.
4. Add the garlic, herbs and cayenne pepper and cook, stirring constantly, for about 30 seconds. Add the chopped tomatoes, tomato purée, stock, reserved shellfish liquor, vinegar, Pepper Sauce and potatoes and bring to the boil, then pop the lid on, reduce the heat and simmer gently, stirring occasionally, until the potatoes are tender, about 20 minutes.

5. Finally, add the prawns, pop the lid back on and cook for about 5-10 minutes, until the prawns are cooked, adding the mussel, clam and cockle meat a few minutes before the prawns are ready, to heat through.
6. Season to taste and serve immediately with chunks of crusty bread.

TWO POTS OR THREE

'Pasteles'

SERVES 6–10

Pasteles (or Hallacas) can be found throughout the Caribbean and South America and are soft cornmeal parcels filled with meat, vegetables and herbs and steamed in a banana leaf. One school of thought is that they were a substitute for the Spanish colonists' empanadas. Traditionally a Christmas food, pasteles are now eaten throughout the year. They can be fiddly to make, and I remember watching Ma like a hawk to learn the encasing technique, so this version gives you all the bang without the buck: a slow-cooked, melt-in-your-mouth ragu and a wet polenta with a sharp, buttery-lemony-garlicky hit. It is a lovely variation on the original and is best eaten with a large dollop of Chow-Chow and a couple drops of Pepper Sauce (see pages 268 and 258).

TIME: 15 MINUTES PREP + 5 HOURS 30 MINUTES COOKING

For the ragu
3–5 tbsp olive oil
1 kg lean stewing steak, cut into roughly 5cm chunks
100g bacon lardons
1½ onions, finely chopped
1½ red peppers, seeded and finely chopped
6 garlic cloves, crushed
3 thyme sprigs, leaves only, finely chopped

3 bay leaves
6 tbsp finely chopped chives
6 tbsp finely chopped flat-leaf parsley leaves
1 x 340g jar pimento-stuffed olives in brine, drained, rinsed, roughly chopped
6 ½ tbsp capers, drained, rinsed, roughly chopped
600ml beef stock
3 tbsp tomato purée
3 tsp Worcestershire Sauce
1½ tsp Pepper Sauce (see page 258)
90ml red wine
4 beef bone marrows
30g flaked almonds, toasted
sea salt and freshly ground black pepper

For the polenta
1 tbsp olive oil
2 garlic cloves, crushed
300ml vegetable stock
150g fine cornmeal
30g butter
zest and juice of 1 lemon
1 tsp finely chopped flat-leaf parsley leaves

1. Pre-heat the oven to 125°C/Gas ½.
2. Heat 2 tablespoons of oil in a large, ovenproof casserole or large pot on a high heat until the oil smokes. Add the steak in batches and brown on all sides. Remove and set aside on a plate for later.

3. Lower the heat to medium, if the casserole is dry add another tablespoon of oil, and add the bacon, onion and peppers and soften for 5 minutes, stirring occasionally. Add the garlic and herbs and cook, stirring continuously, for a minute. Add the remaining ragu ingredients, except for the almonds, give the casserole a good stir and pop it into the oven, covering it with a lid, for 3 hours, giving it a stir every 45 minutes.
4. Reduce the oven temperature to 100°C/Gas ¼, take the ragu out of the oven, give it a good stir and use a wooden spoon to break up the chunks of beef so it begins to fall apart. Pop the uncovered casserole back into the oven for a further 2 hours, stirring, and breaking up the meat a little more every 30 minutes.
5. Remove the casserole from the oven and, using a wooden spoon, break up any remaining chunks of beef. Season to taste, pop the lid back on and set aside. (You can prepare the recipe up to this stage, allow the ragu to cool, then refrigerate for a couple days, or freeze for up to 2 months and defrost before heating up.)
6. To make the polenta, heat the oil in a large saucepan on a medium heat then fry the garlic for about 30 seconds until the wonderful aroma hits you. Add the vegetable stock along with 300ml water and bring to the boil. Gradually whisk in the polenta and continue to whisk until it is smooth, thick and starts to bubble, about 3–5 minutes. Reduce the heat to low, cover the pan and simmer for 10–15 minutes, whisking regularly, until the polenta is cooked through and thick.

7. Stir in the butter, lemon juice and zest and season to taste. Give a final whisk to make sure that the polenta is smooth and not lumpy, transfer to a serving dish and scatter over the parsley.
8. Serve immediately alongside the ragu in the casserole.

Bag-Baked Sea Bass & Black Bean Salsa

SERVES 4-6

This is one of my favourite Euro-Caribbean combos, bringing together the 'al cartoccio' (in-a-bag) method of cooking fish – which keeps it moist, is a healthy way of cooking and locks in the flavours – with the most divine black bean and mango salsa. The potato slices soak up the salty lime flavours in the bag, making them absolutely moreish. This easy-to-make meal is all about light, fresh eating and maximum flavour.

TIME: 15 MINUTES PREP + 40 MINUTES COOKING

3 heaped tbsp virgin coconut oil
800g new potatoes, washed and scrubbed, sliced as thinly as possible
2 x 1kg sea bass, gutted and scaled, rinsed and patted dry
2 unpeeled garlic cloves, smashed
2 limes, thinly sliced
sea salt and freshly ground black pepper

For the black bean salsa
1 x 400g can black beans, drained and rinsed
1 ripe mango, peeled, stoned and chopped into 1cm cubes
1 ripe avocado, peeled, stoned and chopped into 1cm cubes
½ small red onion, finely chopped
1 garlic clove, crushed

½ red chilli, seeded and finely chopped
1½ tbsp finely chopped coriander leaves
½ tsp cayenne pepper
juice of ½–1 lime
1 tbsp virgin coconut oil, melted and cooled (so that it is still liquid but not hot)

1. Pre-heat the oven to 200°C/Gas 6.
2. To make the black bean salsa, gently toss together all the ingredients until just combined and season to taste. Be careful not to over mix, otherwise you will end up with a muddied mush rather than a brightly coloured salsa. Set aside to develop in flavour while you cook the potato and sea bass.
3. Melt the coconut oil in a small saucepan. Place the potato into a large bowl and pour over the melted oil.
4. Lay a large sheet of foil (about 60 x 60cm) on a baking sheet and cover with a piece of parchment paper the same size. Lay the potato slices on top, then bring the edges of the parchment paper and foil up to create a loose bowl around the potato and pour over the excess coconut oil from the bowl and sprinkle with salt.
5. Leaving the parchment paper/foil 'bag' open, pop the baking sheet into the oven for about 15 minutes, turning over the potato halfway through.
6. Score the fish (going deeply into the flesh) in a crisscross pattern, season both sides with salt and pepper and stuff the cavities of the fish with the garlic cloves and half the lime slices. Coat the fish with the melted coconut oil from

the loose foil bowl of potato, then place the fish, side by side, on top of the potato.

7. Top the fish with the remaining lime slices and bring the parchment paper and foil right up over the fish and squeeze the edges together to create a tightly sealed but loose bag. Place the baking sheet with the sealed bag into the oven for about 20-25 minutes, until just cooked (if you slice into the deepest part of the fish, the flesh should no longer be translucent). Remove from the oven and allow to rest (still in the bag) for a few minutes.

8. To serve, carefully remove the foil and place the parchment paper into a shallow serving dish. Loosen the parchment paper, folding back the sides so that everyone can dig in, remove the lime slices from the top of the fish and spoon the salsa over and around the fish. Serve immediately.

Buttermilk Fried Chicken, Biscuits & Milk Gravy

SERVES 4–6

Without a doubt, the Caribbean is a region that appreciates fried chicken! Trinidad apparently has more KFCs per capita than anywhere in the world and a Port-of-Spain branch is the chain's highest-grossing one internationally. (Bear in mind that Trinidad's entire population is about one-sixth of that of London!)

Because I am a little lazy, I love using boneless chicken and it works beautifully, sandwiched between a torn biscuit. If you want to use chicken with the bones in, do, but increase the cooking time. The biscuits recipe is derived from one that Ma used to make for weekend breakfasts. (To clarify: we ate it with scrambled egg rather than fried chicken!)

TIME: OVERNIGHT MARINATING + 30 MINUTES PREP + 30 MINUTES COOKING

For the buttermilk fried chicken
8–10 chicken thighs, boned and skinned
200ml buttermilk
2 free-range eggs, beaten
groundnut oil, for frying
sea salt and freshly ground black pepper

For the seasoning flour
200g cornflour
200g plain flour
8 tsp paprika
4 tsp dried thyme
4 tsp garlic granules
2 tsp sea salt
1 tsp onion powder
1 tsp celery salt
1 tsp cayenne pepper
½ tsp freshly ground black pepper

For the biscuits
225g plain flour, sifted
¾ tbsp baking powder
1 tsp sea salt
pinch of freshly ground black pepper
75g cold vegetable shortening, diced
135ml whole milk
30g butter, melted
pinch paprika

For the milk gravy
20g unsalted butter
2 tbsp plain flour
120ml whole milk
120ml good-quality chicken stock

1. Using a sharp knife, deeply score the chicken pieces. Sprinkle with a little salt and place in a large freezer bag.

Pour in the buttermilk, tie the freezer bag, leaving enough space for the chicken to be moved around in the bag, and massage the buttermilk into all the pieces. Pop it into the fridge to marinate overnight.

2. The following day, pre-heat the oven to 225°C/Gas 7 and line a baking sheet with greaseproof paper.
3. To prepare the biscuits, put the flour, baking powder, salt and pepper in a bowl and stir together, using a fork. Working quickly, use your fingertips to rub the shortening into the flour, lifting it high out of the bowl and letting it fall back in, incorporating air, until the mixture looks like coarse breadcrumbs. (If you wish, you can use a food processor on a pulse setting to do this.) Add the milk gradually, stirring with a fork, until the mixture comes together to form a dough.
4. Tip the dough out on to a lightly floured surface and knead no more than ten times.
5. On a large sheet of greaseproof paper, roll out the dough to about 5mm thick. Use a 6cm round cutter to cut out six circles of dough and place on the prepared baking sheet.
6. Use the melted butter to brush the uncooked biscuits then sprinkle each with a little paprika. Bake for 10–12 minutes, until golden.
7. While the biscuits are cooking, prepare the chicken. Put all the seasoning flour ingredients into a large bowl (big enough to fit a chicken piece) and use a fork to mix until well combined. Place the beaten egg into another large bowl, next to the bowl of seasoned flour, and a large plate next to this. Take a piece of buttermilk-marinated chicken out of the bag, wipe off any excess buttermilk with kitchen

paper and dunk it into the seasoned flour, coating it all over. Tap off any excess flour, dunk into the beaten egg, then back into the flour. Once again, tap off any excess flour, then set aside on the plate. Continue until you have coated all the chicken pieces.

8. Pour groundnut oil into a large, heavy-based saucepan to 1cm deep and heat on a high heat until it reaches 180°C, or a breadcrumb dropped into the oil sizzles and turns golden almost immediately. Set aside a large plate (close to the pan) and line with a few sheets of kitchen paper.

9. When the biscuits are cooked, remove from the oven and place on wire rack to cool. Turn down the oven to its lowest setting.

10. Place the chicken pieces into the oil so each piece is in full contact with the bottom of the pan (you will need to do this in batches). Immediately turn the heat down to the lowest setting, pop the lid on and cook for 4–7 minutes. Using kitchen tongs, turn the chicken over, pop the lid back on and cook for a further 4–7 minutes. Remove the lid, turn the heat right up and fry the chicken until golden-brown, turning frequently. Cut into the deepest piece of chicken to ensure that the juices run clear and that it is cooked through.

11. As each batch of chicken is cooked, place it on to the kitchen-paper-lined plate to remove excess oil, then place in a roasting tin, cover with foil and put in the oven to keep warm while you cook the remaining chicken pieces in the same way.

12. To make the milk gravy, in a small pan, on a low heat, melt the butter, then whisk in the flour to make a smooth roux.

Gradually whisk in the milk and chicken stock, bring to the boil and simmer for a couple minutes, whisking continuously, until thick and gravy-like. Season to taste and decant into a gravy boat.

13. Transfer the chicken pieces and the biscuits onto a large serving plate and serve immediately with the boat of gravy.

Jamaican Beef Patties

MAKES 6–8 LARGE OR 12–16 SMALL PATTIES

These patties are like a tropically charged equivalent of Cornish pasties. There is something so reassuringly homely about them, yet at the same time, when you bite through that short, spiced pastry into the moist, flavour-loaded meat filling, you get a hint of something so exotic. Patties are often stuffed into coco bread to make rather extravagant sandwiches but I prefer mine with a nice fresh salad for an easy dinner or lunch. Make the mini versions for afternoon snacks or party canapés. You can swap out the beef and use lamb or turkey mince instead, or even a mix of diced vegetables; so long as you stick with the spicing, they will not disappoint – my big sister Rhe will attest to this!

TIME: 20 MINUTES PREP + 50 MINUTES COOKING

For the pastry
600g plain flour
3 tbsp Madras curry powder
3 tbsp ground turmeric
330g cold butter, diced
12–16 tbsp ice-cold water
sea salt and freshly ground pepper

For the filling
6 tbsp olive oil
2 onions, finely diced
8 large garlic cloves, crushed
1½ tbsp Madras curry powder
3 tbsp finely chopped thyme leaves
5 tbsp finely chopped chives
600g lean minced beef
240ml beef stock
1 tsp molasses sugar
2 tsp Pepper Sauce (see page 258, or 1 chilli, seeded and finely chopped)
2 slices of bread (wholemeal or white), torn into tiny pieces
1 free-range egg, beaten

1. Pre-heat the oven to 200°C/Gas 6.
2. To make the pastry, sift together the flour, curry powder and ground turmeric into a bowl, add a pinch of salt then transfer to a food processor, add the butter and pulse (or use your fingertips to incorporate) until the mixture looks like coarse sand. Tip the mixture back into the bowl and sprinkle the water evenly over, starting with just 4 tablespoons, and bring the dough together with your fingertips. Gradually add more water, a tablespoon at a time, so that you do not end up with sticky dough. The dough should eventually come together into a ball and leave the bowl clean. Wrap in cling film and chill for 30 minutes. (You can prepare the pastry for this recipe up

to 3 days in advance, if you wish; just bring it back to room temperature before rolling it out.)

3. In the meantime, make the filling. Heat the oil in a medium-sized saucepan on a medium heat. Add the onion and soften with a little pinch of salt for about 5–10 minutes, stirring often. Add the garlic, curry powder, herbs (and if you are using fresh chilli, add this now too) and cook, stirring continuously, until the aroma is released from the pan, about 1 minute.
4. Add the minced beef, breaking it up with a wooden spoon and browning it all over, stirring occasionally, for about 5 minutes. Then add the stock, molasses sugar and Pepper Sauce (if you are using it) and bring to the boil. Reduce the heat, cover with a lid and let the mixture simmer gently for about 10 minutes, stirring now and again.
5. Finally, add the bread, cover the pan and let the mixture continue to simmer for a further 10 minutes, stirring occasionally. Remove the pan from the heat, season to taste and set aside to cool.
6. Remove the pastry from the fridge and roll out, using a flour-dusted rolling pin, on to a large sheet of greaseproof paper to a thickness of about 5mm. (Halve the dough and work in two batches, if easier.) Cut out six to eight 19cm circles (you could use a saucer as a guide) or twelve to sixteen 10cm circles from the rolled pastry.
7. Divide the filling between the circles, spooning it on to one half of each pastry circle, leaving space at the edge to allow for sealing the pastry. Using your fingertip and a little water, wet the edges of the pastry and fold the non-filled

half of the pastry over the filled half and use a fork to press down the edges to seal. (You can prepare this up to 2 days in advance and chill, or freeze for up to 2 months and defrost before cooking, if you wish.)
8. To cook, brush the patties with the beaten egg, pop them on to a baking sheet and bake for about 20 minutes, until the pastry is cooked through and golden.
9. Allow to cool for a couple of minutes before serving.

'Bake & Shark'

SERVES 6

This is my take on a traditional beach food served up at Maracas Bay in Trinidad. Lining up with a cold beer in hand and smelling wafts of the fried shark as you wait in a ridiculously long queue is a blissful memory in itself, let alone actually devouring it! And the table brimming with sauces, chutneys and extras is a testament to a condiment-obsessed nation! Think of it as a burger, but with tropical appeal. But, whatever you do, you must have it with the zingy, garlicky tamarind sauce. Add a couple drops of Pepper Sauce (see page 258), too, if you want to try it the local way.

TIME: OVERNIGHT MARINATING + 20 MINUTES PREP + 10-15 MINUTES COOKING

6 x 75g-130g centre-cut (loin) fillets of white, meaty fish (e.g. cod or pollock), skinned and pin-boned
3 tbsp Green Seasoning (see page 271)
1 litre groundnut oil, for frying
3 free-range eggs, beaten
90g plain flour, for coating
90g panko breadcrumbs, for coating
sea salt and freshly ground black pepper

For the tamarind sauce
6 tbsp mayonnaise
2 tbsp tamarind paste
juice of 1 small lime
5 garlic cloves, crushed
2 tbsp finely chopped coriander
¼ cucumber, finely diced

To serve
6 just-made Fried Bakes (see page 141), or fresh crusty baps
½ iceberg lettuce, shredded
3 beef tomatoes, thickly sliced
Pepper Sauce (see page 258, optional)

1. Place the fish fillets and Green Seasoning into a large plastic freezer bag, seal or tie the bag closed and gently massage until all the fillets are coated in the seasoning. Pop the bag into the fridge to marinate overnight.
2. To make the tamarind sauce, mix together all the ingredients in a small bowl, season to taste and set aside.
3. When you are ready to make the burgers, half fill a wok, or a deep, large saucepan with groundnut oil, and heat to 180°C, or until a breadcrumb immediately sizzles and becomes golden when dropped into the oil. Alternatively, use a deep-fat fryer, following the manufacturer's instructions. Line a plate with kitchen paper and place it near the wok.

4. While waiting for the oil to heat up, set out three medium-sized bowls (large enough to easily dunk a fillet into). In one bowl place the beaten egg, in the next, the flour, and in the last, the panko breadcrumbs. Wipe off any excess marinade from the fish fillets and dip each one firstly into the flour then, having gently shaken off any excess, into the egg and finally into the panko, ensuring that the fillets are well coated. Set aside while you crumb the remaining fillets.
5. Gently place the fillets into the hot oil (you may need to do this in batches of two or three, depending on the size of your pan) and fry until crisp and golden-brown and the fish is cooked through (if you slice into it, the flesh should no longer be translucent), about 4–6 minutes, flipping them over halfway, if necessary. Remove with a slotted spoon and rest on the kitchen-paper-lined plate while you fry the remaining fillets.
6. To serve, simply open the bake, or bap, pop in some shredded lettuce, a couple of slices of tomato and the crispy fish, smother with the tamarind sauce (and a little dotting of Pepper Sauce too, if you fancy) and enjoy immediately.

Buljol Butties

SERVES 4–6

As I am writing this, I am tucking into a Buljol Butty for breakfast while sheltering under a shady umbrella in Tobago! This is a common breakfast dish, but also works well without the Fried Bakes as a light saltfish salad. I highly recommend serving it with this spicy aïoli and slices of buttery soft avocado, which, while perhaps not totally authentic, is a really yummy combination.

TIME: OVERNIGHT SOAKING + 10 MINUTES PREP + 15 MINUTES COOKING

750g salt cod, or other saltfish
2 spring onions, bulb removed, finely chopped
2 large vine tomatoes, seeded and finely chopped
1 yellow (or orange) pepper, seeded and finely diced
2 tsp finely chopped chives
3 tsp lime juice
½ tbsp extra virgin olive oil
sea salt and freshly ground black pepper
4–6 Fried Bakes (see page 141), to serve
1 ripe avocado, peeled and stone removed, thinly sliced, to serve

For the aïoli
4 heaped tbsp mayonnaise
4 garlic cloves, crushed
2–4 tsp Pepper Sauce (see page 258) depending on how hot you like it, or 1 finely chopped red chilli
½ tsp paprika

1. Submerge the salt cod in water and soak for 12 hours, or overnight, changing the water five or six times.
2. Rinse the salt cod, place in a large saucepan, cover with fresh water and bring to the boil. Once the water begins to boil, remove the pan from the heat, drain the boiled water, add fresh cold water and bring to the boil again. As soon as the water starts to boil, reduce the heat and simmer for about 5–10 minutes, until the salt cod is cooked through. Drain the water and set the salt cod aside to cool.
3. When the salt cod is cool enough to handle, flake the meat of the fish into a bowl, discarding pin bones and skin. Use two forks to go over the fish, flaking it finely.
4. Gently but thoroughly incorporate the spring onion, tomato and pepper, then add the chives, lime juice and olive oil and season to taste.
5. To make the aïoli combine all the ingredients well in a bowl. Taste and adjust the seasoning as necessary.
6. To serve, slice open the Fried Bakes, spread liberally with the aïoli, stuff with the salt-cod mixture, and top with slices of avocado.

Baked Eggs Creole

SERVES 6

This has to be one of the greatest brunch dishes ever – chilli and eggs are a heaven-made match – and is particularly useful for those occasions when you are perhaps a little fuzzy-headed from the night before and have to throw together something tasty at the last moment and with minimal effort. For something a little meatier, add slices of cooked sausage or chorizo to the sauce. Serve with slices of toast.

TIME: 15 MINUTES PREP + 35 MINUTES COOKING (INCLUDES MAKING THE SAUCE)

1 portion Sauce Creole (see page 266)
300g spinach
12 free-range eggs
olive oil, for drizzling
sea salt and freshly ground black pepper

1. Pre-heat the oven to 200°C/Gas 6.
2. Make the Sauce Creole (see page 266). On a gentle heat, add the spinach gradually, stirring often, until wilted.
3. Pour the Sauce Creole into a wide, large ovenproof dish (you may need to use two), and spread evenly over the base. Make 12 little wells (or six, if using two dishes) in the sauce and break the eggs into each well. Drizzle each egg

with a little oil and sprinkle with a pinch of salt and black pepper, cover with foil or a lid and pop into the oven for about 10–15 minutes, or until the whites are just set and serve immediately.

Corned Beef & Cabbage

SERVES 4-6

I remember absolutely loathing corned beef and cabbage as a child, yet now I fully embrace, even crave it! This mouth-wateringly tasty, brunch/lunch/dinner recipe is low cost to make and thoroughly fulfilling – and anything topped with a soft-centred fried egg is a winner in my eyes! If you don't want to eat it with rice, serve with Fried Bakes (see page 141, or, if you're really taking it easy, fluffy rolls), as served at Rosie's in Tobago – breakfast to go!

TIME: 5 MINUTES PREP + 35 MINUTES COOKING

500g plain white or brown rice, rinsed
30g unsalted butter
3 tbsp olive oil, plus extra for egg frying
2 large onions, thinly sliced
1 tsp granulated sugar
½ tbsp sherry vinegar
½ medium-sized cabbage, finely shredded
1 red pepper, seeded and diced
2 tbsp Green Seasoning (see page 271)
1 tbsp tomato ketchup
½ tsp Pepper Sauce (see page 258)
½ tsp paprika
4-6 large free-range eggs

500g corned beef, in large, thick flakes, at room temperature
sea salt and freshly ground black pepper

1. Cook the rice in boiling salted water, according to the packet instructions, then drain and set aside.
2. In the meantime, heat the butter and 2 tablespoons of the oil in a large saucepan on a low heat until the butter has melted. Add the onion, a small pinch of salt and the sugar and stir often, until the onion softens, about 10 minutes.
3. Add the vinegar and the remaining tablespoon of oil and continue to cook until the onion is browned and caramelised, about 10 to 15 minutes.
4. Remove the caramelised onion with a slotted spoon and set aside on a small plate.
5. Increase the heat to medium and add the cabbage and pepper to the oil remaining in the pan. Give it a quick stir, pop the lid on the pan and cook for 2–5 minutes, stirring regularly, until the cabbage has just softened.
6. Add the Green Seasoning, ketchup, Pepper Sauce and paprika, stir to combine evenly with the cabbage, and cook for a further 5 minutes or so, with the lid off, stirring occasionally.
7. In the meantime, fry the eggs in a large frying pan in a little oil, with a pinch of salt and pepper, until the whites are cooked to your liking and the yolk is runny.
8. Take the pan of cabbage off the heat, add the reserved caramelised onion and gently stir in the corned beef to heat it through. Season to taste.
9. Serve immediately with the rice and topped with a fried egg.

Cou-Cou & Fish

SERVES 6

Cou-cou and flying fish is the national dish of Barbados. Cou-cou is a seasoned, wet polenta studded with okra and it works well with rich sauces like Sauce Creole (see page 266), which soaks into it beautifully. The crisp-skinned fish is meaty and savoury and it contrasts beautifully with the sweet cou-cou and Sauce Creole. You can use any meaty fish – try cod or pollock – and the cou-cou also makes a great accompaniment for other meat or vegetable dishes that are steeped in a rich sauce. It is said that if a man finds lumps in his cou-cou he can throw his wife out of the house. Evidently, the point here is that you should beat the hell out of that cou-cou until it is silky smooth!

**TIME: 1 HOUR MARINATING
+ 15 MINUTES PREP + 40 MINUTES COOKING**

For the fried fish
6 tilapia fillets (or other white, mild-flavoured fish fillets), skin lightly scored
2 tbsp Green Seasoning (see page 271)
2 large garlic cloves, crushed
1 tsp cayenne pepper
1 tsp paprika
1–2 tbsp olive oil

25–50g butter
sea salt and freshly ground black pepper

For the cou-cou
1 tbsp olive oil
1 large onion, finely chopped
4 garlic cloves, crushed
4 thyme sprigs
½ tbsp finely chopped coriander leaves
100g okra, stems removed, thinly sliced
400ml freshly boiled water
400ml vegetable stock
200g fine cornmeal
40g unsalted butter
pinch of grated fresh nutmeg
1 quantity of chunky Sauce Creole (page 266), to serve
melted butter, to serve

1. Place the tilapia fillets in a bowl and massage in the Green Seasoning, garlic, spices and a pinch of salt and pepper. Leave to marinate, flesh-side down, in the fridge for 1 hour before cooking.
2. To make the cou-cou, heat 1 tablespoon of oil in a large saucepan on a medium heat, add the onion and soften with a little pinch of salt for about 5 minutes, stirring often.
3. Add the garlic, thyme and coriander and cook for about 30 seconds, stirring continuously, until the wonderful aroma hits you. Stir in the okra and sauté for a minute, then add the 400ml freshly boiled water and bring to the boil.

Reduce the heat to low and simmer for 10 minutes. With a slotted spoon, remove the okra and set aside on a plate for later.

4. Add the vegetable stock to the pan, turn up the heat and bring to the boil. Whisk in the polenta gradually, and continue to whisk until it is smooth, thick and starts to bubble, about 3–5 minutes. Reduce the heat to low, cover the pan and simmer for 10 minutes, whisking very often, until the polenta is cooked through, thick and smooth. Stir in the okra, so that it is well combined. Remove the thyme sprigs and discard. Add the butter and nutmeg and season to taste.

5. While the polenta is cooking, fry the fish. Heat a large frying pan on a high heat, add a tablespoon of oil and fry the fillets, skin-side down, for 3–4 minutes, or until the skin is crisp and golden brown. Flip the fillets over, add half the butter to the pan and continue to fry for 2–3 minutes, or until cooked through, basting them in the butter as it melts. You may need to fry the fish in batches, depending on the size of your pan.

6. To serve, gently reheat the Sauce Creole. Scoop a generous serving spoon of the cou-cou on to a plate. Place the fish on top and then pour over the sauce. Serve immediately.

For the barbecue

The cou-cou can be prepared as per the recipe above. The fish fillets need to be about 2.5cm thick, to survive barbecuing (haddock works very well here if you can't get tilapia that's thick enough). Once you are ready to cook the marinated fish, pre-heat the barbecue until the coals have just turned white. Ensure that the grates of the barbecue are clean and well oiled. Melt the butter and liberally brush the fish fillets on both sides. Pop the fillets, skin-side down, perpendicular to the grate, on to the hottest part of the barbecue, then pop the lid on and cook for about 3-4 minutes, until the skin is crisp and charred. Carefully flip the fish over, using a fish slice to gently coax the fillet off the grate and cook for another 3 minutes or so, until the fish has turned white and is just cooked. Allow it to rest under tented foil for a few minutes before serving as above.

SOMETHING ON THE SIDE

Fried Bakes

MAKES 6 BAKES

I know how contradictory a 'Fried Bake' may sound, but I suppose there is some sort of logic behind it: frying the bakes at a hot temperature seals the outside and bakes, or rather steams, the inside. These are sometimes referred to as johnny cakes or dumplings and are crispy on the outside and fluffy on the inside with oodles of flavour. If you have never tried them, you are in for a really special treat. You can have them at any time of the day, with any meal and they are exceptionally good for soaking up sauces. Sometimes I just like them hot out of the pan, sliced open with a little cheese and some Pepper Sauce (see page 258). They're best served immediately!

TIME: 10 MINUTES PREP + 30 MINUTES RESTING + 15 MINUTES COOKING

360g self-raising flour, sifted
good pinch of salt
20g butter, at room temperature
150–200ml water
a little olive oil, for coating
groundnut oil, for frying

1. Whisk together the flour and the salt in a large bowl then use your fingertips to rub the butter into the flour until it resembles fine breadcrumbs. Gradually add the water (you may not need to use all), mixing with a spoon, until a dough forms.
2. Tip the dough out on to a lightly floured surface, rub your hands with a little oil and knead, for about a minute or so, until smooth then form into a ball. Pour a drop of oil on to your palm and coat the dough. Cover it in cling film and leave it to rest for 30 minutes in a warm place.
3. Return the dough to a floured surface and knead a few more times. Divide the dough into six balls and flatten each into a palm-sized circle. Use your fingertips to coat the top of each ball with a little oil.
4. Pour the groundnut oil into a large wok, or high-sided saucepan, so that it comes halfway up. (If using a deep-fat fryer, follow the manufacturer's guidelines.) Heat the oil to 180°C: when you pop a breadcrumb in it should sizzle and turn golden brown almost immediately. Line a large plate with kitchen paper and set this down near the pan.
5. Pop the raw bakes into the hot oil – two or three at a time, depending on the size of your wok – and fry them for about 30 seconds to a minute, until they start to puff up. Flip them over and fry for a further 30 seconds to a minute. Continue to flip them over and cook until they are golden and puffy on both sides. Remove with a slotted spoon and place onto the kitchen-paper-lined plate to soak up any excess oil. Serve immediately.

Coconut Rice & Peas

SERVES 6–8

Each Caribbean island has its own take on this little dish. I love the bite and slight stickiness of brown rice but you can use white rice if you prefer; you will just need to reduce the cooking time to about 20 minutes. I've taken liberties and have studded the rice with pomegranate seeds and fried lime peel: both bring a great tang to the dish and cashew nuts add a pleasant crunch but leave them out if you fancy it traditional. This is a fantastic accompaniment to grilled, baked or barbecued meats and fish, but it also makes a lovely, light dinner: just stir through a little cooked veg at the end.

TIME: 10 MINUTES PREP + 50 MINUTES COOKING

3 tbsp virgin coconut oil
1 onion, finely chopped
2 garlic cloves, crushed
½ tsp ground allspice
500g brown rice, rinsed
1 x 400ml can coconut milk
600ml vegetable stock
½ x 160ml can coconut cream
1 thyme sprig
1 x 400g can kidney beans, drained and rinsed
1 Scotch bonnet pepper, unpierced and unbruised

2 limes
olive oil, to fry
60g toasted cashew nuts, roughly chopped
seeds from 1 pomegranate
sea salt and freshly ground black pepper

1. Heat the coconut oil in a large pan on a low heat, add the onion and a little salt and soften for about 5 minutes, stirring regularly. Add the garlic and allspice and cook for about 30 seconds, stirring continuously, until the aroma is released, then add the rice and stir until the grains are well coated.
2. Add the coconut milk, stock, coconut cream, thyme and a good pinch of salt, give it a stir, bring to the boil and cook for 20 minutes with the lid on. Add the kidney beans and the Scotch bonnet pepper, reduce the heat to a simmer and continue to cook for a further 20–25 minutes, with the lid on, until the rice is just tender and the liquid is absorbed. (You may need to add a little boiled water to the pan if necessary to allow the rice to cook fully.)
3. In the meantime, zest the limes using a citrus zester (or use a vegetable peeler and slice the peel into 1mm strips). Pour the olive oil into a small pan to about 5mm deep and heat on a high heat until the oil reaches 180°C: when you pop a breadcrumb in it should sizzle and turn golden brown almost immediately. Line a small saucer with kitchen paper and set this down near the pan.

4. Add the lime zest to the hot oil and fry for a few seconds, until crispy, then remove with a slotted spoon and set aside on the lined saucer.
5. Remove the thyme sprig and the Scotch bonnet from the rice, fluff with a fork and season to taste.
6. Finally, gently fold through the cashew nuts, pomegranate seeds and lime zest and serve immediately.

Spiced Sweet Potato Wedges

SERVES 5-8

This simple recipe makes a perfect addition to lunches and dinners during all seasons. Try chopping and changing the flavouring by using garlic granules, cayenne, chilli powder or just straight up salt and pepper. Potato wedges are wonderful for dunking: serve them with Pineapple Ketchup, Molasses and Rum Barbecue Sauce and garlic mayo laced with Pepper Sauce (see pages 262, 260 and 258).

TIME: 10 MINUTES PREP + 45 MINUTES COOKING

1kg sweet potato, scrubbed, skin on, cut into wedges
3 tbsp olive oil
1 tsp ground cumin
1 tsp paprika
sea salt and freshly ground black pepper

1. Pre-heat the oven to 200°C/Gas 6.
2. Pop the potatoes wedges into a freezer bag with the oil, cumin, paprika and a pinch of salt and pepper, then seal the bag and shake it and turn it upside down to fully coat the potato wedges.
3. Lay the wedges out in a single layer on a baking sheet (you may need to use two) and bake for 40-45 minutes, until

crispy and cooked through, giving the baking sheet a shake every 15 minutes to ensure even cooking.
4. Season to taste and serve.

For the barbecue
Pre-heat the barbecue until the coals just turn white. In the meantime par-boil the wedges, in salted water for about 5-7 minutes, until just cooked but still firm. Allow to cool, pat the wedges dry with paper towel and then season the wedges, as per step 2 above. Pop a batch of the wedges on to the grate over the hottest part of the barbecue and cook for about 1 minute, turning halfway through, until charred on both sides. Repeat with the remaining wedges. Season to taste and serve.

Buss-Up Shut

SERVES 6

This roti (also called paratha) differs from a usual roti as its texture is flaky – a little more 'buttery' – and it is bashed up with a rolling pin (or bailna, as we call it) before serving. The name 'buss-up shut' came to be when a local Trini decided that the roti resembled a ripped-up, or burst shirt – pronounced there as 'buss-up shut'. You could eat this by itself or use it to dip into chokas, curry or anything saucy really.

TIME: 45 MINUTES PREP + 45 MINUTES RESTING + 30 MINUTES COOKING

240g plain flour, plus extra for dusting
2 tsp baking powder
1 tsp sugar
1 tsp sea salt flakes
olive oil, to rub
softened ghee

1. Mix together the flour, baking powder, sugar and salt in a large bowl and then add about 200g/7fl oz water (you may not need to add it all), kneading for a few minutes to make a very soft pliable dough. Rub the dough with oil, place in a bowl, cover, then rest for 30 minutes.

2. Divide the dough into 4 balls. Take one of these balls and roll it out on a lightly floured surface to the size of just smaller than the base of a large frying pan. Brush the roti very, very generously with ghee.
3. Take a knife and cut from the centre to the edge of the circle (a radius line). Take the cut edge and roll it around, following the line of the radius of the circle, so you end up with a cone, and tuck in any loose pieces under and all the way in to keep the cone together. Stand the cone up, then flatten it and push the tip of the cone all the way down with your thumb. Repeat with the remaining 3 balls and leave to rest for at least 4 hours, loosely covered.
4. Heat a large, heavy-based frying pan on a high-medium heat and, using a heat-proof brush, brush the base with ghee.
5. Roll out one of the pieces of dough again on a flour-dusted surface to the size of just smaller than the base of the frying pan (make sure the edges are thin too). Carefully pop it into the hot pan and brush the surface of the roti with more ghee. Then flip the roti over, and brush the other side with ghee.
6. Cook for a few more minutes, flipping when you get a golden-brown colour on the underside, with little touches of brown. Take tongs, or two wooden spatulas, and crush or beat the roti gently so it flakes up and the layers separate a little, taking in the edges to the centre. The roti should be flaky at the top, but soft inside. Pop into a clean, dry tea towel to keep warm while you do the same with the remaining 3 pieces of dough.

Mashed Green Bananas

SERVES 4-6

This dish is usually made with green figs, which are like bananas, but never turn yellow: they remind me of an earthy variety of potato. Outside of the Caribbean, I use firm, green, unripe bananas, and they work just as well. Even though this is a side dish and goes stonkingly well with a little cooked fish and a rich sauce, I sometimes enjoy it as a light dinner, with a pinch of grated nutmeg mixed through and served with a little wilted spinach.

TIME: 5 MINUTES PREP + 20 MINUTES COOKING

8 green, unripe bananas
3 large garlic cloves, crushed
leaves of 1 large thyme sprig
1 tbsp olive oil
4 tbsp double cream, warmed
1 tsp finely chopped chives
a teensy pinch of ground nutmeg
sea salt and freshly ground black pepper

1. Score a line down the length of each banana skin. Put the bananas into a large pan, cover with cold, salted water, bring to the boil and cook for about 15-20 minutes, until the

bananas are tender and a knife can easily pierce the skin. Drain the bananas and set aside until cool enough to peel.
2. In a pestle and mortar, make a paste with the garlic, thyme leaves and a pinch of salt.
3. Heat 1 tablespoon of the olive oil in a small frying pan and fry the paste on a low heat, stirring, for about 15 seconds, until the earthy aroma is released.
4. Mash the bananas with the paste and 2–4 tablespoons of the warm cream until smooth. Add the chives and nutmeg and season to taste. Serve immediately.

Bacon-Studded Pumpkin Talkari

SERVES 4-6

Talkari is a word taken from our Indian heritage and basically means a side dish, usually a little mashed. My all-time favourite talkari, and the most common when I was growing up, was pumpkin. This recipe really reminds me of a pumpkin purée, full of warm earthiness from the spice, bacon lardons and fried shallot.

TIME: 10 MINUTES PREP + 20 MINUTES COOKING

400g peeled pumpkin, cut into small chunks
1½ tbsp olive oil
100g bacon lardons
1 shallot, finely chopped
2 garlic cloves, crushed
¼ tsp ground cumin
2½ tbsp double cream
¼ tsp grated fresh nutmeg
sea salt and freshly ground black pepper

1. Cook the pumpkin in a saucepan of salted boiling water on a medium heat until tender, about 10–15 minutes.
2. In the meantime, heat ½ tablespoon of the oil in a frying pan on a medium heat and fry the bacon lardons until crisp. Set aside until cool.

3. In the same frying pan, heat the remaining tablespoon of oil and soften the shallot, with a pinch of salt, for about 5 minutes. Add the garlic and cumin and cook for 30 seconds, stirring continuously until the aroma is released. Set aside.
4. In a large bowl, roughly mash the pumpkin with the double cream, then add the nutmeg and stir until well mixed. Stir in the bacon lardons, fried shallot and garlic, season to taste and serve immediately.

Pineapple & Peanut Slaw

SERVES 4-6

A slaw with a difference: the subtle sweetness of the pineapple balances the gentle heat from the cayenne and chilli while the peanut adds great crunch (add as much or as little as you like). This slaw is great with barbecued meats, deli hams and cheeses, and for picnics. To make it lighter, replace half the mayo with Greek yoghurt. To ensure that the slaw retains its bite, make this no more than a few hours before serving.

TIME: 20 MINUTES PREP + 1 HOUR 15 MINUTES SOAKING + DRAINING

- ½ large red cabbage, roughly shredded, soaked in cold water for 15 minutes
- ½ small white onion, finely shredded
- 1 large carrot, peeled, quartered then peeled lengthways into ribbons
- 1 red chilli, seeded and finely sliced lengthways
- 150g fresh pineapple, cored and cut into small chunks
- pinch of cayenne pepper
- pinch of paprika
- pinch of dried oregano
- 3-6 tbsp mayonnaise
- handful of peanuts, toasted and roughly chopped

1 tbsp chopped coriander leaves
sea salt and freshly ground black pepper

1. In a large bowl, toss the cabbage, onion and carrot with the chilli and pineapple. Stir the cayenne, paprika and oregano into 3 tablespoons of the mayonnaise then toss with the slaw, ensuring it is fully coated. Add more mayonnaise, and toss well, until you have the desired creaminess of slaw. Season to taste and mix one final time to combine. (You can prepare the recipe up to this stage and chill for a few hours, tossing again before serving).
2. Sprinkle over the peanuts and coriander and serve.

Doved Peas

SERVES 6-8

This is sort of a Caribbean version of the classic combo ham and peas. The earthiness of the gungo peas and thyme here are perfect with the salty, smoky ham hock and bacon. This is such a quick dish to whip up and although it makes an obvious side dish, you could also serve it as a cracking light dinner with any cooked grains stirred through it. Any leftovers make for a fab lunch.

TIME: 5 MINUTES PREP + 10 MINUTES COOKING

15g butter
100g bacon lardons
1 large onion, finely chopped
2 garlic cloves, crushed
2 thyme sprigs, plus ½ tsp finely chopped thyme leaves
2 x 400g cans gungo peas
½ tsp Pepper Sauce (see page 258) or ¼ small chilli, seeded and finely chopped
60g cooked ham hock, shredded
sea salt and freshly ground black pepper

1. Heat half of the butter in a large frying pan on a medium heat and fry the bacon lardons until crisp. Remove with a slotted spoon and set aside on a small plate.

2. Add the remaining butter to the frying pan, heat until it has melted and soften the onion, with a small pinch of salt, stirring often, for about 5 minutes.
3. Add the garlic and thyme (and fresh chilli, if using) and cook for about 30 seconds, stirring constantly, until the aroma is released. Stir in the gungo peas, the hot sauce and finally the ham hock. Heat until warm, about 3 minutes, then gently stir in the crispy bacon.
4. Remove the thyme sprig, stir through the thyme leaves, season to taste and serve immediately.

Kale Bhaji

SERVES 4-6

Bhaji is a sautéed dish, usually made from callaloo leaves or dasheen leaves (dasheen is a wild, more 'intense' form of spinach). I make it with kale so that it retains a little more body. In the Caribbean you would find this on the table for not only lunch and dinner, but for breakfast, too. Stirring through some cooked mixed beans turns this into a tasty, healthy light lunch.

TIME: 5 MINUTES PREP + 15 MINUTES COOKING TIME

3 tbsp olive oil
1 large onion, finely chopped
2 large garlic cloves, crushed
50g coconut cream
1 small Scotch bonnet pepper, unpierced and unbruised
200g kale, washed and chopped
sea salt and freshly ground black pepper

1. Heat the oil in a large saucepan on a low heat. Add the onion and a small pinch of salt and soften, stirring often, for about 5 minutes.
2. Add the garlic, creamed coconut and Scotch bonnet and gently stir until the creamed coconut has melted. Then add the kale, cover the pan and cook for 5 minutes.

3. Remove the lid and continue to cook for a further couple of minutes, stirring occasionally, until any liquid has evaporated.
4. Remove from the heat, discard the Scotch bonnet (or chop a little of it up and mix it in), season to taste and serve.

'Fry Bodi'

SERVES 4-6

Bodi is a long green bean growing in the Caribbean that is similar to string/green beans that are common in the UK, but a lot longer. Bodi fried in a little tomato, onion and garlic is commonly eaten for breakfast, but I think they work brilliantly as an accompaniment to meat or fish served at dinner or lunch. With the addition of some boiled new potatoes and nutty olive oil, this makes a great light meal, too.

TIME: 5 MINUTES PREP + 15 MINUTES COOKING

1 tbsp olive oil
15 very ripe cherry tomatoes, roughly chopped
½ onion, finely chopped
2 garlic cloves, crushed
200g string beans, trimmed
sea salt and freshly ground black pepper

1. Heat the oil in a large saucepan on a medium heat. Add the tomatoes and onion and soften, stirring often, for about 5 minutes. Add the garlic and give it a stir, cooking for a further 30 seconds, until the aroma hits you. Finally add the string beans, cover the pan and cook, stirring occasionally, until the beans are tender, about 5-10 minutes. Season to taste and serve.

SWEET THINGS

Coconut Soufflé & Hot Buttered Rum

SERVES 4-6

This angelic, delicately scented coconut soufflé is cloud-light and beautifully balanced by the utterly devilish hot buttered rum. And not only is it delicious, it is actually a doddle to make – this soufflé simply doesn't fall – the coconut milk works structural magic! What with the spices, the rum, the lime and the coconut, you could be forgiven for thinking you were reclining on white sands under a blue sky, cocktail in hand!

TIME: 20 MINUTES PREP + 15 MINUTES COOKING

For the coconut soufflé
30g unsalted butter, melted
60g caster sugar (for dusting the ramekins)
1 x 400ml can coconut milk
1 tsp coconut syrup (available online or from certain off-licences)
2 tbsp plain flour
2 tbsp cornflour
zest of 1 lime
6 free-range eggs, at room temperature, separated
generous pinch of cream of tartar
110g caster sugar
20g icing sugar, for dusting

For the hot buttered rum
60ml double cream
60g salted butter
110g granulated sugar
4 tbsp good-quality dark rum
generous pinch of ground cinnamon
generous pinch of grated fresh nutmeg

1. Pre-heat the oven to 180°C/Gas 4. Measure out all your ingredients and have them ready and close to hand. Brush the inside of four to six 9 x 5cm individual ramekins thoroughly with the melted butter and coat with the caster sugar, gently tapping off any excess.
2. In a small saucepan on a low heat, whisk together the coconut milk, coconut syrup, plain flour, cornflour and lime zest until thickened and custard-like, about 4 minutes. Allow to cool for a couple of minutes.
3. Place the egg yolks into a mixing bowl and beat in the thickened milk mixture until combined. Cover with foil and keep in a warm place. (You can prepare this up to a day in advance, chill and just reheat gently to room temperature before continuing with the rest of the recipe, if you wish.)
4. In another mixing bowl, whisk the egg whites with an electric whisk until frothy. Add the cream of tartar and then, continuing to whisk, add the caster sugar gradually until the mixture forms stiff peaks.
5. Vigorously beat a quarter of the egg whites into the coconut mixture, to lighten it. Fold in the remaining egg whites in two batches, quickly, but gently, using a large spatula or

wooden spoon. Do not over fold – it doesn't at all matter if the mixture is a bit streaky.
6. Pour the mixture into the prepared ramekins and level off the tops with a palette knife, or the non-serrated side of a standard knife. Use your clean little finger to trace a line around the inner edge of each dish to separate the soufflé from the rim to help the soufflés rise straight. Place the ramekins on a baking sheet and pop in the oven for about 7–10 minutes, until risen and golden brown, but still with a bit of a jiggle when gently nudged.
7. In the meantime, make the hot buttered rum. Stir the cream, butter and sugar in a small pan on a low heat until the sugar dissolves and the sauce is smooth, about 5–8 minutes. Do not let it boil.
8. Stir in the rum, cinnamon and nutmeg and pour into a jug. Set aside, stirring occasionally to prevent a film forming on the top.
9. When the soufflés are ready, gently remove them from the oven, dust lightly with the icing sugar and serve immediately with the hot buttered rum ready to pour into the pierced soufflés.

Mango Mojito Granita

SERVES 4–6

A tropically refreshing end to any meal. The mangoes need to be really ripe to lend their natural creaminess to this very simple iced treat. The mint and lime act as a lovely palate-cleanser that could easily make this granita a simple 'shot-glass' course between a main course and dessert. The granita is just as sublime without the rum, but its addition does makes it that little bit more tropical (well, that's my excuse, anyway!).

TIME: 10 MINUTES PREP + 7 HOURS FREEZING

3 soft, ripe mangoes, peeled, stone removed and flesh roughly chopped
zest and juice of 1½ limes
12 mint leaves, roughly chopped, plus 6 small mint sprigs, to decorate
4½ tbsp good-quality dark rum
caster sugar, to taste

1. In a large bowl, using a stick blender, blitz the mango, lime juice and zest and the mint leaves until smooth.
2. Add the rum, give a stir and if needed, add caster sugar, to taste.
3. Pour the mango 'mojito' into a freezable container and place in the freezer for about 7 hours, until solid.

4. About 3–5 minutes before serving, remove the granita from the freezer to defrost it a little, then use a fork to scrape it until you get a light fluffy texture all the way through. Scoop this into martini or shot glasses and top with a small mint sprig. Serve immediately.

Grenadine Orange Salad

SERVES 4-6

This salad makes a great dessert when you want something quick, light and healthy – perfect for a balmy, summer's day. Grenadine syrup is a commonplace ingredient in many Caribbean punches and is originally a pomegranate-derived syrup, although now it is more of a 'red berry' syrup. I've scattered pomegranate (in homage to the original syrup) over the salad which also adds a pleasant sharpness and crispness. The light mint and the warm nutmeg add beautiful layers that complete this refreshing dessert.

TIME: 10 MINUTES PREP + 15 MINUTES 'DEVELOPING'

5 large juicy oranges
2 tbsp grenadine syrup
pinch of grated fresh nutmeg
1 tbsp finely chopped mint leaves, plus a few small whole leaves to decorate
seeds of 1 pomegranate

1. To peel and remove the pith from the oranges, firstly roll an orange on a flat surface to 'loosen' the fruit. Cut both ends off the orange so that it can stand upright. Using a sharp knife, carefully cut away at the peel and the pith, following

the curve of the orange as carefully as possible. Do the same with the remaining oranges. Slice the orange horizontally into 5mm discs. Repeat with the remaining oranges.
2. Place the orange slices in a bowl, along with any juices, pour over the grenadine syrup and sprinkle over the pinch of nutmeg. Gently toss with your hands to combine then place in the fridge for 15 minutes so that the flavours soak into the orange. (You can prepare the recipe up to this stage in advance if you wish: it will keep for up to 2 days in the fridge.)
3. Just before serving, gently toss through the pomegranate seeds and the chopped mint. Decorate with the mint leaves.

Pineapple Chilli Crème Brûlée

SERVES 6

What is more satisfying than cracking the top of a scorched crème brûlée with the back of your spoon? Well, I suppose eating it! The pineapple in this recipe adds a little lightness to the luscious creaminess that you would expect from a crème brûlée, making it a refreshingly light way to end a meal. I especially love the hint of warmth from the chilli and cinnamon.

TIME: 20 MINUTES PREP + 1 HOUR 10 MINUTES COOKING + 3 HOURS COOLING

300g fresh pineapple, cored and cut into small chunks
450ml double cream
¾ tsp ground cinnamon
dash of good-quality vanilla extract
zest of ½ lime
1-2cm red chilli, seeded and very finely chopped
8 free-range egg yolks
180g caster sugar, plus extra for sprinkling

1. Pre-heat the oven to 150°C/Gas 2.
2. Using a stick blender, blitz the pineapple until puréed and smooth.
3. Heat the double cream, puréed pineapple, cinnamon and vanilla extract in a small saucepan on a medium heat,

stirring regularly, until the mixture starts to bubble, about 3–5 minutes.
4. Remove the pan from the heat and strain the mixture through a sieve (using the back of a spoon to help push the cream through) into a jug. Stir in the lime zest and chilli.
5. In a large bowl, beat the egg yolks and sugar together until pale and fluffy and then stir in the pineapple cream.
6. Bring a small pan of water to a constant simmer. Place the bowl of pineapple cream and egg mixture on the pan, ensuring that the bottom of the bowl doesn't come into contact with the water. Continue to whisk gently for about 10 minutes over the heat, until the mixture has thickened a bit. Remove any froth on the surface and set aside.
7. Place six 7.5cm-diameter ramekins into a large, high-sided roasting tin. Create a bain-marie by carefully pouring just-boiled water into the tin until it reaches halfway up the outside of the ramekins. Ladle the thickened pineapple cream mixture into the ramekins until they are two-thirds full. Place the roasting tin into the oven and bake for 45–50 minutes, until the creams are set, but with a jelly-like wobble in the centre.
8. Carefully remove the ramekins from the bain-marie and let cool completely before chilling for about 3 hours, until firm. (You can prepare the recipe up to this stage and chill for up to 2 days in advance.)
9. Sprinkle a thin layer of caster sugar over the chilled, set creams and swirl the ramekin around so that the sugar covers the entire surface, gently tapping off any excess.

Use a blowtorch (moving the flame in a constant circular motion), or pop under a high grill for a few seconds, to caramelise the sugar completely. Allow the crème brûlées to cool and their surfaces to harden for a couple minutes, then serve.

Poached Pawpaw & Vanilla Whip

SERVES 4-6

I love how delicately perfumed papaya is and the way that it almost melts away in the mouth. I never want to overpower it, so I find that poaching it in a gently spiced liquor is one of the best ways to show it off it in a refined, but simple dessert. When the vanilla whip and poaching liquor combine on your spoon, the flavours are so reminiscent of a mellow spiced rum, you may well think that someone has spiked the saucepan! If you want to make this even lighter, leave out the cream and icing sugar and just serve the pawpaw with generous dollops of coconut yoghurt, or Greek yoghurt, studded with the vanilla seeds.

TIME: 5 MINUTES PREP + 15 MINUTES COOKING + 2 HOURS COOLING

500ml freshly boiled water
200g demerara sugar
5 cloves
1 cinnamon stick, broken in half
3 large, just ripe, firm (not over-ripe or soft) papayas, peeled, seeded and cut into large (2cm) chunks
zest of 1 lime plus the juice of ½ thumb-sized piece of fresh root ginger, peeled

For the vanilla whip
2 vanilla pods, split in half lengthways
200ml double cream
200g coconut-milk yoghurt, or Greek yoghurt
1 tbsp icing sugar
4-6 mint sprigs, to decorate

1. Put the boiled water in a large pan with the sugar, cloves and cinnamon and heat on a medium heat, stirring regularly, until the sugar has dissolved.
2. Turn the heat down low, add the papaya, lime zest and juice and ginger and poach on a very gentle simmer, ensuring that the papaya is always submerged, for about 10 minutes (allow 5 minutes if the papaya is softer and 15 minutes if it is very firm), until just tender but still holding shape. Set aside to cool to room temperature.
3. To make the vanilla whip, use the point of a sharp knife to scrape the seeds from the vanilla pod into a mixing bowl. Add the cream and icing sugar and whip until soft peaks form when the whisk is removed.
4. In a separate bowl, take a large tablespoon of the whipped cream and stir vigorously into the yoghurt until it has loosened a little. Gently fold this yoghurt mixture back into the whipped cream. Chill in the fridge until needed.
5. To serve, remove the cloves and cinnamon from the poaching liquor. Divide the papaya between individual dessert or wine glasses, spoon over some of the poaching liquor, top with the vanilla whip then a sprig of mint.

Double Ginger Chocolate Mousse

SERVES 6

Considering that Trinitario cacao, from Trinidad, is one of the three main cacao bean varieties used in chocolate, I felt it would be sacrilege to not have a chocolate-based dessert in a Caribbean cookbook! And this cocoa nib-topped chocolate mousse fits the bill perfectly: not only is there the earthiness of the ground ginger through the chocolate but there is also a surprise of a tiny fire-bomb of candied ginger at the bottom that lingers in your mouth after the last bite. It is important to use good-quality chocolate (even if it isn't of Caribbean origin!). This is a perfect dinner-party dessert: it's easy to prepare in advance and is sophisticated, too.

TIME: 5 MINUTES PREP + 50 MINUTES COOKING + 3 HOURS SETTING

For the candied ginger
70g fresh root ginger, peeled and roughly cut into 5mm cubes
80g plus 6 tsp granulated sugar

For the dark chocolate and ginger mousse
200g good-quality dark chocolate (70% cocoa solids), broken into small shards
2 tsp ground ginger

pinch of salt
6 free-range eggs, separated, plus 2 egg whites
pinch of cream of tartar
40g golden caster sugar
1 tbsp cocoa nibs, roughly chopped

1. To make the candied ginger, submerge the ginger cubes in a small saucepan of boiling water and continue to boil for about 40 minutes, until the ginger cubes are tender, topping up with water to ensure that the ginger remains submerged.
2. Line a baking sheet with greaseproof paper.
3. In the meantime, make the chocolate and ginger mousse. Place a heatproof bowl over a small pan of simmering water (on a low heat), ensuring that the bottom of the bowl doesn't come into contact with the water. Put the chocolate into the bowl, along with the ground ginger and a pinch of salt, and gently melt the chocolate, giving it an encouraging stir with a spatula every now and again. Once the chocolate has melted, remove from the heat and allow to cool slightly.
4. In a separate bowl, whisk the egg yolks until thick and creamy then beat into the melted chocolate until smooth. Set aside.
5. Drain the boiling ginger, then place back in the pan along with the 80g of sugar and fill with fresh water so that the ginger is just covered with water. Bring to the boil and reduce the heat to a low simmer, stirring often, until the water has evaporated and you are left with an almost dry pan of frothy sugar syrup.

6. Transfer the candied ginger to the lined baking sheet, sprinkle over the extra sugar and leave to cool for about 10–15 minutes.
7. Once cool enough to handle, break up any pieces of ginger that are stuck together and divide between six martini glasses, or dessert bowls, reserving a very small amount to garnish.
8. In a separate, clean bowl, whisk all the egg whites until frothy. Add a pinch of cream of tartar and continue to whisk, gradually adding the sugar, a spoonful at a time, until soft peaks form when the whisk is removed from the egg whites. (Don't over whisk or you will get a very dense mousse.)
9. Vigorously mix a third of the egg whites into the melted chocolate and egg yolk mixture to loosen it. Then gently fold in the remaining egg whites until just combined, with no trace of white.
10. Spoon the mousse into the six glasses, cover with cling film and chill for about 3 hours, until set.
11. Just before serving, scatter over the cocoa nibs and a tiny amount of the reserved candied ginger.

Salted Tamarind Caramel Sundae

SERVES 6-8

Just looking at this sundae makes me feel like a child again! It works so well because the salted tamarind caramel balances out the sweetness of the condensed-milk ice cream and leaves a lovely, tangy aftertaste on the tongue, while the crunch from the cashew nuts offers a pleasant textural contrast to the smooth, velvety ice cream. Making the popcorn is entirely worth it as it is so easy, as is the ice cream, which is no-cook and no-churn. Indeed, it sometimes bewilders me how such wonderful results can come from so little work!

TIME: 10 MINUTES PREP + 1 HOUR 30 MINUTES COOKING + 6 HOURS FREEZING

1 tbsp virgin coconut oil
25g popping corn
40g unsalted cashew nuts
6-8 maraschino cherries, to serve

For the salted tamarind caramel
150g caster sugar
90g salted butter
150ml double cream
2 tbsp tamarind concentrate
large pinch of sea salt

For the ice cream
1 x 397g can condensed milk
300ml double cream

1. Pre-heat the oven to 120°C/Gas ½ and line a small baking sheet with greaseproof paper.
2. Heat the coconut oil in a large saucepan on a medium heat. Add the popping corn, cover the pan and give it a good shake. After a few minutes, the corn will begin to pop, occasionally at first and then more frequently – keep shaking the pan on the heat. Once the popping sound tails away, remove the pan from the heat and carefully remove the lid. Watch out for the odd kamikaze popcorn!
3. To make the salted tamarind caramel, ensure that you have the butter and double cream close to hand. Heat the sugar in a wide saucepan on a very low heat. As it begins to melt in small areas, swirl the pan to move the dry sugar into the molten patches, but do not stir. After about 15 minutes, when most of the sugar is molten and dark brown in colour (don't worry if there are a few hard chunks of sugar in the mix, as long as it is no longer white sugar), use a metal spatula to vigorously stir in the butter, until roughly incorporated, then stir in the cream and continue mixing on a low heat, working at breaking down any large chunks of caramel, until the liquid is smooth. At this stage stir in the tamarind and the salt and set aside to cool a little.
4. To make the ice cream, whisk the condensed milk and the double cream until thick and fluffy and an indentation remains if you poke it with your finger.

5. Pour the whipped cream mixture into a large plastic container and carefully, a spoonful at a time, fold in half of the tamarind caramel so that it is dispersed throughout the ice cream in ripples. Pop into the freezer for 6 hours or so, until it reaches a soft but firm ice cream consistency.
6. While you wait for the ice cream to freeze, you can make the tamarind caramel popcorn. Spread the popcorn and the cashew nuts out on to the prepared baking sheet. Pour over enough of the remaining salted tamarind caramel to ensure that the popcorn and cashews are well coated. You can use a spoon to help you mix the caramel through. Spread the mixture out a little then place in the oven for 1 hour, giving it a stir every 15 minutes.
7. Remove the baking sheet from the oven and leave to cool to room temperature and harden up. Break up any large pieces that have clumped together and store in an airtight container until needed, for up to a week.
8. Serve the ice cream in bowls and top generously with the tamarind caramel popcorn and a maraschino cherry. You can be extra decadent and spoon on some leftover salted tamarind caramel too, if you wish!

Banana Tarte Tatin

SERVES 6

I go monkeys for banana puddings, and the combination of creamy banana, crisp, light pastry and sumptuous buttery caramel is just the best! The other reason to love a banana tarte Tatin is that it is super simple to make and yet sounds so complex. It's a definite crowd-pleaser, particularly when served with a scoop of vanilla ice cream or a little whipped cream, but make sure you serve it immediately so that the pastry doesn't go soggy.

TIME: 20 MINUTES PREP + 1 HOUR COOKING

- 200g caster sugar
- 100g salted butter, diced
- dash of good-quality vanilla extract
- dash of Angostura bitters
- 6 very ripe (some dark spotting) bananas, peeled and halved lengthways
- ¼ tsp ground cinnamon
- ¼ tsp grated fresh nutmeg
- small pinch of allspice
- 300g ready-to-roll, all-butter puff pastry
- plain flour, for dusting
- zest of ½ lime
- vanilla ice cream or whipped cream, to serve (optional)

1. Pre-heat the oven to 180°C/Gas 4.
2. Heat the sugar and butter in a large ovenproof frying pan on a medium heat, stirring continuously for about 15-20 minutes until the mixture is golden, the sugar has dissolved and it smells like caramel.
3. Stir in the vanilla extract and Angostura bitters, then lay the bananas tightly side by side in the pan to cover the base. You may need to break some of the banana halves into smaller pieces to fit around the pan. Be very careful to not burn yourself on the hot caramel. Sprinkle over the cinnamon, nutmeg and allspice and set aside.
4. Place the pastry on its thinnest edge on a lightly floured surface and roll out to a thickness of about 5mm. Using a sharp knife, carefully cut out a large circle, a little larger than the base of the frying pan. Carefully, draping the pastry circle over the rolling pin to help lift it, place the pastry on top of the bananas and gently tuck the excess around the edge of the pan, ensuring that the bananas are all fully covered.
5. Pop the frying pan into the oven and bake for about 35-40 minutes, until the pastry is golden, crisp and cooked through.
6. Remove the pan from the oven, let it rest for a few minutes, then carefully place a large plate upside down on top of the frying pan, turn the whole thing over and carefully ease the tart out of the pan and on to the plate. Sprinkle over the lime zest, cut into slices and serve immediately with a scoop of vanilla ice cream or a dollop of whipped cream.

Pumpkin Lava Cake & Black Pepper Cardamom Custard

SERVES 6

Pumpkin is an important staple in the Caribbean and is versatile enough to use in sweet dishes as well as savoury. I made this once as an alternative to chocolate fondant cake and what a lucky thing that was! It is a foolproof, gooey-in-the-middle, spiced thing of beauty that is superbly enhanced by the earthy aromatics of the to-die-for custard. One of my favourite comfort puds ever!

TIME: 30 MINUTES PREP + 20 MINUTES CHILLING + 15 MINUTES COOKING

For the lava cakes
150g unsalted butter, at room temperature
150g light brown sugar
150g fresh pumpkin purée
3 free-range eggs, beaten
45g golden syrup
90g plain flour
1 tsp ground cinnamon
1 tsp ground nutmeg
1 tsp ground ginger
⅓ tsp ground cloves
⅓ tsp ground allspice
⅓ tsp ground black pepper

For the black pepper cardamom custard
250ml whole milk
250ml double cream
½ tsp ground green cardamom
a generous dash of good-quality vanilla extract
6 free-range egg yolks
75g caster sugar
large pinch of freshly ground black pepper

1. Pre-heat the oven to 200°C/Gas 6.
2. Melt 60g of the butter and brush the inside of six dariole moulds (5cm high and 8cm diameter). Chill until the butter has set then brush a little more melted butter over the set layer and place back in the fridge until needed.
3. In a small bowl, cream the remaining butter with the sugar, then gradually mix in the pumpkin purée, beaten egg and golden syrup.
4. In a separate bowl, sift the flour and spices together and gradually beat this dry mix into the wet pumpkin mix. Divide the batter between the six dariole moulds and chill for 20 minutes.
5. In the meantime, make the black pepper cardamom custard. Heat the milk and cream with the cardamom and the vanilla extract in a small saucepan on a moderate-to-low heat, stirring regularly, until it starts to bubble gently. Remove from the heat and set aside to infuse the flavours for 5 minutes.
6. In a bowl, beat the egg yolks and caster sugar together until pale and fluffy then whisk in the cardamom cream mixture and pour back into the pan. Place on a low heat

and, stirring continuously, heat the custard until it thickens enough to coat the back of a spoon and a line drawn through it remains.
7. Remove from the heat, add the pepper and keep warm.
8. Pop the lava cakes on to a baking sheet and bake in the oven for about 10–15 minutes, until risen and with a little bit of wobble.
9. Carefully turn out the cakes on to individual plates and serve hot with the warm custard.

Watermelon Sherbet

SERVES 4-6 (MAKES ABOUT 700ml)

Both the colour and texture of this dessert remind of me of bubblegum, but the flavour is undeniably, juicily and deliciously watermelon. A sherbet is something between a sorbet and an ice cream, if we are talking dairy content. If you prefer to leave out the natural food colouring, you can of course do so: the sherbet will be a little paler, but just as divine!

TIME: 20 MINUTES PREP + 30 MINUTES CHILLING + 45 MINUTES-6 HOURS FREEZING (SEE METHOD)

4 gelatin leaves
600g seeded, ripe, watermelon flesh
1 tbsp lime juice
75g caster sugar
pinch of salt
100ml double cream
2 tbsp good-quality white rum
1 tsp natural red food colouring

1. Soak the gelatin leaves in cold water for 5 minutes.
2. In the meantime, blitz together the watermelon, lime juice, sugar and a pinch of salt in a food processor until smooth. Pour the mixture into a mixing bowl and set aside.
3. Squeeze out any excess water from the gelatin and, in a small saucepan on a low heat, dissolve it in 100ml of water, stirring.
4. Add the dissolved gelatin mixture to the watermelon mixture, along with the double cream, rum and food colouring. Stir until well combined, then pop it into the fridge to chill for 30 minutes.
5. When the watermelon mixture is cool, transfer it to an ice-cream maker and freeze according to to the manufacturer's instructions. Alternatively, transfer the mixture to a small freezable container with a lid and freeze for an hour then remove from the freezer and use a fork or electric whisk to really churn through the sherbet, breaking up the ice crystals so that the mixture is the same consistency. Pop it back into the freezer for another 2-3 hours, whisking it about every half an hour, then lay a sheet of cling film against the surface and freeze until as firm as ice cream.
6. The sherbet will keep for up to 2 months in the freezer. Before serving, allow it to defrost for about 15-20 minutes, until soft, then scoop into little dessert bowls and serve immediately.

Pineapple Fritters with Lime Caramel & Rum Whipped Cream

SERVES 6–8 (MAKES ABOUT 12–18 FRITTERS)

You really need super sweet, almost overripe, pineapples for this, but having said that, their slight natural tartness makes them a perfect candidate for 'frittering', in which they are contrasted with the crisp, sweet batter. I have added a little drizzle of lime caramel, which adds a zesty-sweetness. Of course you don't have to add rum to the whipped cream – you could replace it with a sprinkle of nutmeg. A word of warning when enjoying it: don't be too impatient, wait for it to cool a little as the fritters are as hot as the surface of the sun! You could also try this recipe with ripe bananas.

TIME: 25 MINUTES PREP + 30 MINUTES COOKING TIME

2 small, ripe pineapples, peeled, cored and sliced into 1cm-thick rings
groundnut oil, for frying
sea salt

For the rum whipped cream
600ml double cream
1½ tbsp icing sugar
3 tbsp good-quality dark rum

For the lime caramel
200g caster sugar
50g salted butter, cubed
180ml double cream
zest of 1 lime plus juice of ½

For the batter
2 free-range eggs, separated
175g plain flour, sifted
75g cornflour
2 heaped tsp baking powder
75g golden caster sugar
300ml coconut milk
15g unsalted butter, melted
pinch of cream of tartar

1. To make the rum whipped cream, whip the double cream with the icing sugar, until soft peaks form then gently fold in the rum. Set aside in the fridge.
2. To make the lime caramel, dissolve the sugar in a saucepan on a low heat, stirring continuously. Once the sugar has fully dissolved, add the butter and, once it has melted, stir in the cream, lime zest and juice and a good pinch of salt and continue stirring until smooth, on a low heat. Keep warm, otherwise it will solidify. (If you want to make it in advance, simply reheat on a low heat before serving.)
3. To make the batter, beat the egg yolks in a small bowl. In a large mixing bowl, whisk together the plain flour, cornflour, baking powder, sugar and a pinch of salt until fully combined. Make a well in the centre and pour in the

coconut milk, beaten egg yolks and melted butter. Whisk to combine the wet and dry ingredients until you have a smooth batter.

4. Pour the oil into a wok or high-sided pan so that it comes a third of the way up and heat to 180°C: when you pop a breadcrumb in it should sizzle and turn golden brown almost immediately. (If using a deep-fat fryer, follow the manufacturer's instructions.) Line a plate with a few sheets of kitchen paper and set aside close by.
5. Using an electric whisk, whisk the egg whites with the cream of tartar until stiff peaks form. Genty fold this into the batter.
6. Pat a pineapple ring dry with a sheet of kitchen paper, dip it into the batter until well coated, gently let any excess batter drip off then place it into the hot oil. Fry until golden, about 3–5 minutes, then remove with a slotted spoon and place on the kitchen paper to soak up any excess oil. Repeat with the remainder of the pineapple rings.
7. Drizzle the pineapple fritters liberally with the caramel and serve immediately with a generous dollop of the rum cream.

Smashed Banana Pancakes

SERVES 4-6 (MAKES ABOUT 8-12 PANCAKES)

These tropical pancakes are crisp on the outside and fluffy on the inside and are rather like a version of the French toast my pa would make for us. My go-to topping would either be slathering these in a mixture of Nutella and rum or in maple syrup with berries and bacon – delicious!

TIME: 10 MINUTES PREP + 20 MINUTES COOKING

25g self-raising flour, sifted
½ tsp baking powder
¼ tsp ground cinnamon
2 tbsp chocolate chips
pinch of sea salt
4 large, overripe bananas, roughly mashed with a fork
1 tbsp maple syrup
3 small free-range eggs, beaten
2 tbsp coconut yoghurt, or Greek yoghurt
½ tsp vanilla extract
3 free-range egg whites
pinch of cream of tartar
virgin coconut oil, for frying

1. In a small bowl, whisk together the flour, cinnamon, chocolate chips and salt until well combined.
2. Place the mashed banana in a separate, large bowl, along with the maple syrup, then stir in the flour mixture then the beaten eggs, yoghurt and vanilla extract until well combined.
3. In a separate bowl, whisk the egg whites with a pinch of cream of tartar until soft peaks remain when the whisk is removed.
4. Mix a quarter of the egg whites into the banana mixture then gently fold in the remainder.
5. In a large frying pan, on a medium heat, heat a tablespoon of coconut oil, tilting the pan to ensure the oil covers the base. Ladle out a little of the batter (about 4–5 tablespoons) and tilt around the pan so that the batter forms roughly a 10cm pancake. Cook until the pancake is golden and dry underneath, about 30 seconds to a minute, then flip over and cook for a further 30 seconds to a minute, until the pancake is cooked through. Repeat with the remaining batter and serve immediately with a topping of your choice.

Snow Cones

SERVES 6–10

Snow cones are one of those little treats that, when I was a kid and the sun was out, I would go absolutely mad for: messy, brightly coloured and packed with sugar! As I have grown up, I have realised that this thing of iced beauty is actually one of the most simple sweets to make and, depending on how you top it, can be as healthy (or naughty) as you like!

TIME: 10 MINUTES PREP + 2 HOURS CHILLING

500g ice cubes

For 'milk' syrup
60g dried skimmed milk powder
60g granulated sugar
100ml boiling water
40ml coconut cream
55g unsalted butter, melted
2 drops of good-quality vanilla extract
½ tsp grated fresh nutmeg
½ tsp ground cinnamon
8 tbsp milk

For 'red' syrup
flesh of ½ large watermelon, seeded
6 tbsp grenadine
2 tbsp sugar syrup

For 'golden' syrup
10 passion fruit, seeds and pulp only
zest of 1 lime
1 ripe mango, peeled and stone removed
6 tbsp passionfruit syrup

1. To make the milk syrup, pop all the ingredients except the milk into a blender and blitz until the sugar has dissolved and the mixture is smooth. Allow to cool completely before chilling for a couple of hours in the fridge. Before serving, stir in the milk so that the consistency is a little more runny but still syrupy.
2. To make the red syrup, pop all the ingredients into a blender and blitz until combined, then chill for a couple of hours in the fridge.
3. To make the golden syrup, pop all the ingredients into a blender and blitz until combined, then chill for a couple of hours in the fridge.
4. Just before you are ready to serve, pulse the ice cubes, in small batches, in a food processor until shaved and fluffy. Scoop immediately into bowls and drench in the syrup of your choice to enjoy at once.

Passion Lime Meringue Pie

SERVES 8–10

This mixture of crisp sweet pastry, creamy tangy filling and marshmallowy meringue is heavenly! The passion fruit makes a pleasant addition to the classic lime filling and has a natural tartness that eventually flowers into sublime tropical sweetness. This is a great prepare-ahead dessert that has real wow factor and actually isn't at all difficult to make.

TIME: 35 MINUTES PREP + 50 MINUTES CHILLING + 50 MINUTES COOKING + 1 HOUR COOLING

For the pastry
220g plain flour
120g cold unsalted butter, diced
1 tbsp icing sugar
pinch of sea salt
1 free-range egg, beaten
a little egg white, for brushing

For the passion fruit and lime filling
150g fresh passion fruit pulp and seeds (roughly 7 passion fruit)
70g cornflour
60ml lime juice (roughly 6 limes), strained
zest of 1 lime

1 x 397g can condensed milk
4 free-range egg yolks, beaten
pinch of sea salt

For the meringue
5 free-range egg whites, at room temperature
large pinch of cream of tartar
170g caster sugar
2 level tsp cornflour

1. Grease a 23cm-diameter loose-bottomed fluted flan tin. Set aside.
2. To make the pastry, put the flour, butter, icing sugar and salt into a food processor and pulse until the mixture looks like coarse sand. Add the beaten egg and a tablespoon of ice-cold water and pulse until the mixture begins to bind together. Tip the dough out into a bowl and bring together with your fingertips. The mixture should leave the bowl clean and there should be no dry flour remaining. Wrap the dough in cling film and chill for 30 minutes. (You can prepare the pastry for this recipe 3 days in advance if you wish.)
3. Place a baking sheet (large enough to contain the flan tin) into the oven and pre-heat the oven to 200°C/Gas 6.
4. On a large sheet of greaseproof baking paper, roll the chilled dough out just thinly enough to fully line the base and sides of the tin, with a little extra for overhang. Gently but quickly flip the greaseproof paper over onto the tin, peel off the paper and press the pastry into the base and fluted sides of the tin, gently pressing the overhang over the rim. Prick the base of the pastry a few times with a

fork, ensuring not to go all the way through, then line the pastry with foil, shiny side down and pop into the freezer for 20 minutes.

5. Fill the foil-lined tin with dry beans, place in the oven on the pre-heated baking sheet and blind-bake for about 15 minutes. Carefully remove the foil and beans, and use a sharp knife, at an angle, to cut the overhang from the side of the tin. Place the pastry case back in the oven for a further 10 minutes, or until pale golden and dry. Brush the pastry lightly but thoroughly with the egg white and pop it back in the oven for a further minute, until dry, to seal the pastry. Remove and set aside. Lower the oven temperature to 180°C/Gas 4.

6. In the meantime, make the filling. Reserve 2 tablespoons of the passion fruit pulp and seeds and set aside. Pass the remaining passion fruit pulp and seeds through a sieve using the back of a spoon to push through as much juice as possible. Return this to the pulp and seeds. (You should have about 90g of combined fruit/pulp/seed mixture.)

7. Make a paste with the cornflour and lime juice and, using a balloon whisk, whisk in the passion fruit mixture, lime zest, condensed milk, egg yolks and the salt until smooth.

8. Pour the filling into a sauce pan and cook on a low heat, stirring constantly, until thickened, about 3–5 minutes. Pour the filling into the pastry case and allow it to cool whilst you make the meringue.

9. To make the meringue topping, whisk the egg whites, using an electric whisk on a low-medium speed, until frothy. Add the cream of tartar and then gradually add half the sugar, whilst continuously whisking at a medium-high

speed. Add the cornflour and the remaining sugar and whisk until stiff peaks form.
10. Spoon the meringue gently on top of the filling: beginning at the edges so that it just touches the pastry, spread it into the centre and then continue to pile on and swirl the meringue in large billowy clouds in the centre.
11. Pop the pie into the oven and bake for 15–20 minutes, until the meringue is gold-tinged and cooked through.
12. Leave to cool completely, carefully remove the pie from the tin, then slice generously and serve, or store in the fridge for up to 3 days.

Peanut Butter Cheesecake with Grape Jelly

SERVES 8–10

Because of its proximity to the USA, the Caribbean is heavily influenced by its fads in fashion, music and food. When I was growing up, amongst all the local dishes, the odd one or two USA-inspired ones crept in, most memorably peanut butter and jelly – always grape flavoured – which we would eat on crackers for a wee afternoon snack. And I admit that I still regularly treat myself to this. Now I am not about to give you a recipe breaking down the art of the perfect PB and J crackerwich. Instead, here is a simple no-bake cheesecake that captures the flavour of this common playground lunch. Don't expect sickly sweetness, though: this is actually a little salted and quite grown-up (although I expect that kids will go mad for it too!).

TIME: 10 MINUTES PREP + 40 MINUTES COOKING + OVERNIGHT SETTING

For the grape 'jelly'
1kg black seedless grapes, washed and stalks removed
200g caster sugar
100ml water

For the cheesecake base
150g digestive biscuits

75g salted peanuts
1 tbsp golden caster sugar
150g unsalted butter, melted

For the cheesecake
300g cream cheese
200g smooth peanut butter (preferably with no added sugar)
100g soured cream
200g double cream
40g icing sugar

1. To make the grape 'jelly', place the grapes into a large sauce pan with the sugar and water, stir and leave for 10 minutes.
2. Bring the mixture to a boil and continue boiling, stirring regularly and using a wooden spoon to crush the grapes, for 40–50 minutes, until reduced and thickened to a compote consistency. Set aside to cool.
3. To make the cheesecake base, in a food processor, blitz together the digestive biscuits, peanuts, sugar and the butter until the mixture clumps together and falls off the sides of the processor into the centre.
4. Line a 20cm spring-form cake tin with greaseproof paper. Using the back of a spoon, firmly press the mixture into the base as evenly as possible. Pop into the fridge to firm up for an hour whilst you make the filling.
5. To make the filling, beat together the cream cheese, peanut butter and soured cream until well combined and uniform in colour.

6. In a separate bowl, whisk the double cream with the icing sugar until soft peaks remain when the whisk is removed. Gently fold this into the peanut butter mixture until well incorporated.
7. Pour the filling on to the biscuit base and use a spatula to gently smooth and spread it evenly. Return the cheesecake to the fridge to set overnight. (You can prepare the cheesecake in advance, if you wish: it will keep in the fridge for up to 3 days.)
8. When you are ready to serve it, carefully release the cheesecake from the tin. Slice generously, and serve the slices topped with the grape 'jelly'.

STICKY-FINGERED GOODIES

Sweet Potato Pone

MAKES ABOUT 12 SQUARES

The spiced perfume of this tasty traybake wafting from the oven takes me back to my school days. The word 'pone' originally came from the Native Americans and refers to a cornmeal-based bread. In the Caribbean, we make pone with cassava, a root vegetable, but sometimes we throw in sweet potato, too. The texture is pretty unique: it is sticky, supple and soft, with a wee crunch at the edges – just perfect with a cup of tea, or to have hot out of the oven with custard. My husband reckons it's a mash-up of a sweet-potato pudding, a flapjack and a moist carrot cake, complemented by the lovely use of spices. He's hit the nail on the head!

TIME: 10 MINUTES PREP + 45–60 MINUTES COOKING

250g sweet potato, peeled and coarsely grated
150g demerara sugar
90g fine cornmeal
40g desiccated coconut
¾ tsp ground mixed spice
½ tsp ground ginger
½ tsp ground cinnamon
½ tsp freshly ground black pepper
¼ tsp ground nutmeg

¼ tsp ground cloves
pinch of sea salt
100ml coconut milk
25g unsalted butter, melted
½ tsp good-quality vanilla extract
50g raisins

1. Pre-heat the oven to 180°C/Gas 4 and line the base of an 18 x 24cm baking tin with non-stick baking parchment.
2. In a large bowl, mix together the sweet potato, demerara sugar, cornmeal, desiccated coconut, spices, salt, coconut milk, melted butter and vanilla extract until smooth and even, then stir in the raisins.
3. Pour the batter into the baking tin, and using a spoon or spatula, spread out evenly over the base. Place in the oven and bake until golden in colour and a skewer poked into the centre of the pone comes out clean, about 45 minutes to 1 hour.
4. Let the pone rest for 5 minutes before carefully cutting it into squares and transferring to a wire rack to cool completely. Store in an airtight container for up to 5 days.

Buccaneer's Shortbread

MAKES 8-10 BARS (OR 24-30 SMALL SQUARES)

I don't think I've ever met anyone who doesn't love a little millionaire's shortbread – how can you go wrong with caramel, chocolate and shortbread? Here's a sun-drenched version: spiced coconut shortbread, subtly salted caramel with a decadent drizzle of dark rum and a mix of milk and plain chocolate to finish it off. This makes a perfect treat served with a shot of aged dark rum, but my favourite way to enjoy it is with a mug of builder's brew in the afternoon.

TIME: 15 MINUTES PREP + 25 MINUTES COOKING + 2 HOURS COOLING

For the spiced coconut shortbread
140g unsalted butter, softened
60g golden caster sugar
200g plain flour, sifted
55g desiccated coconut
½ tsp ground cinnamon
½ tsp ground nutmeg

For the rum salted caramel
1 x 397g can condensed milk
150g unsalted butter
3 tbsp golden syrup

50ml good-quality dark rum
½ tsp sea salt

For the chocolate topping
125g good-quality dark chocolate (70% cocoa solids), broken into pieces
125g good-quality milk chocolate, broken into pieces
pinch of sea salt

1. Pre-heat the oven to 180°C/Gas 4. Line a baking tin (roughly 30cm x 20cm) with non-stick parchment paper.
2. To make the spiced coconut shortbread, use a wooden spoon to cream together the butter and sugar until light and fluffy.
3. In a separate bowl, mix together the flour, desiccated coconut and spices. Fold this dry mixture into the creamed butter and sugar until it resembles coarse breadcrumbs. (Try not to overmix, otherwise the shortbread won't be nice and crumbly.)
4. Tip the shortbread mixture into the lined tin and evenly flatten it out, using the back of the spoon to compact the mixture into the tin. Place the tin in the oven and bake for about 15 minutes, until the shortbread is pale golden in colour. Set aside to cool on a wire rack.
5. To make the rum salted caramel, put the condensed milk, butter, golden syrup, rum and salt into a small saucepan and bring the mixture to a boil, stirring continuously. Reduce the heat and simmer, still stirring, until the mixture starts to turn a light caramel colour and has thickened a little, about 5–10 minutes. Remove the caramel

from the heat, allow to cool slightly, then pour over the shortbread and leave to cool.

6. To make the chocolate topping, melt both the chocolates in a heatproof bowl, along with the pinch of salt, over a pan of simmering water (ensuring that the bottom of the bowl doesn't come into contact with the water). Give it an occasional stir until the chocolate has melted. Pour the melted chocolate over the caramel shortbread and leave to set for a couple hours.
7. Slice into bars or squares and serve, or store in an airtight container for up to a week to enjoy later.

Salt & Spice Brittle

SERVES 4-6

This makes me think of Ma's special treat, a peanut brittle bar that was always to be found in the glove compartment of the car and which would tempt me something silly on the school run! I have added pumpkin seeds to this brittle as they work so well with the peanut and add a tinge of wholesomeness to an otherwise naughty, epically crunchy treat that is so well-loved in the Caribbean.

TIME: 10 MINUTES PREP + 20-30 MINUTES COOKING

40g salted butter, at room temperature
¾ tsp grated fresh nutmeg
¾ tsp ground cinnamon
large pinch of salt
150g salted peanuts
50g pumpkin seeds
450g caster sugar

1. Pre-heat the oven to 200°C/Gas 6. Line a 17 x 23cm baking sheet with greaseproof paper. Have the butter, spices and salt ready next to the hob, as you will have to work quickly.

2. Roast the peanuts and pumpkin seeds on a baking sheet in the oven, for a couple of minutes, until slightly toasted with a nutty aroma, and set aside.
3. Heat the sugar in a large saucepan on the lowest heat. As it begins to melt in small areas, swirl the pan to move the dry sugar into the molten patches. Do not stir. After about 20–30 minutes, when most of the sugar is molten and dark brown in colour (don't worry if there are a few hard chunks of sugar in the mix, as long as it is no longer white sugar), use a metal spatula to vigorously stir in the butter, spices and salt.
4. Working quickly, take the pan off the heat and vigorously stir in the peanuts and pumpkin seeds, ensuring that they are coated in the caramel.
5. Tip the molten brittle out on to the prepared baking sheet and use the metal spatula to press into the middle of the brittle to flatten it and then push and spread out the edges to form a sheet that just covers the bottom of the baking sheet and is about 5mm thick. Leave to cool completely.
6. After about an hour, when the brittle is fully cooled and at room temperature, crack the surface with a rolling pin so you end up with bite-sized (and a few larger) shards of brittle. Store in an airtight container for up to a week.

Black Cake

MAKES TWO 20cm CAKES

Black Cake is the Caribbean version of a fruitcake, with some distinct differences: it is as rum-soaked as a pirate and is almost pudding-like and sticky in texture, ridiculously moist, dense and highly aromatic. Chop and change the dried fruit as you desire. You can also cover it in marzipan and fondant icing if you like. We tend to make this in bulk, so if you are making it anyway, you may as well make two, but feel free to halve the recipe and make just one. It will keep for up to three months (we came across one after six months, though, and it was heavenly) if you give it a generous 'feed' of rum after it has been baked (although I've never tested this theory as it tends to get eaten – or it leaves the kitchen in doggy bags – in a week or so in my house). Although it is usually a Christmas treat, there is always an excuse to have it year round.

TIME: 20 MINUTES PREP + 5 DAYS SOAKING + 2 HOURS COOKING

500g pitted prunes
500g currants
250g dried pitted cherries
150g raisins
100g candied citrus peel
500ml cherry brandy

500ml good-quality dark rum, plus extra to brush
1 tbsp Angostura bitters
500g demerara sugar
100ml freshly boiled water
400g self-raising flour
100g ground almonds
2 tsp baking powder
2½ tsp mixed spice
zest of 1 lemon
500g unsalted butter, at room temperature
500g caster sugar
8 free-range eggs
2 tsp good-quality vanilla extract
2 tsp almond essence

1. Put all the dried fruit in a large bowl and pour over the cherry brandy, rum and Angostura bitters. Cover with a lid, or cling film and set aside in a cool, dark place to soak for 5 days, giving it a stir every day.
2. Once the fruit has soaked, pre-heat the oven to 150°C/Gas 2 and line two 20cm loose-bottomed cake tins with greaseproof baking paper.
3. Heat the demerara sugar in a saucepan on a medium heat until it dissolves fully and turns a dark caramel colour. At this stage, gradually stir in 100ml of freshly boiled water. Reduce the heat and continue to stir until it is of a syrupy consistency with no sugary lumps.
4. Transfer the fruit (including any leftover alcohol) to a food processor and blend a little, keeping a few chunks throughout.

5. In a large bowl, mix together the self-raising flour, ground almonds, baking powder, mixed spice and lemon zest until well combined.
6. In another large bowl, use a wooden spoon to cream together the butter and sugar until light and fluffy, then incorporate the eggs, one at a time, then the vanilla extract and almond essence. Gradually fold in the dry ingredients, until fully combined, then fold in the blended fruit and the caramelised-sugar syrup.
7. Pour half the batter into each cake tin and pop into the oven for about 2 hours, or until a skewer inserted into the centre of the cake comes out clean. Remove from the oven and allow to cool for 20 minutes.
8. Brush the top of the cakes generously with as much of the leftover dark rum as you fancy (it can really take it), bearing in mind the more you brush on, the more pudding-like in texture the cake will become. Allow the rum to soak in and cool completely before slicing to serve or storing in an airtight container in a cool, dark cupboard for up to 3 months.

Chunky Monkey Cake

SERVES 6–8

This recipe is perfect for using up bruised and blackened bananas that are a little past their prime. It is an amped-up version of a Caribbean favourite, banana bread, packed with pecans and sprinkled with spice. I actually made it for a best friend's wedding and it went down a storm. The luscious and subtle coconut frosting complements the moist banana cake and makes it an ideal afternoon treat, although I confess to sometimes tucking into a thin slice in the morning, too.

TIME: 15 MINUTES PREP + 40 MINUTES COOKING + 30 MINUTES CHILLING

For the banana cake
250g plain flour
1 tsp baking powder
1 tsp bicarbonate of soda
1 tsp ground cinnamon
1 tsp ground nutmeg
¼ tsp ground allspice
¼ tsp ground ginger
pinch of sea salt
275g light brown sugar
155g unsalted butter
2 free-range eggs, beaten

400g (peeled weight) overripe (bruised and black) bananas, peeled and mashed
75ml buttermilk
½ tsp good-quality vanilla extract
75g pecans, toasted and roughly chopped

For the coconut frosting
300g icing sugar
60g unsalted butter
130g cream cheese
½ tbsp coconut syrup or essence (available online or from certain off-licences)
40g desiccated coconut, lightly toasted

1. Pre-heat the oven to 170°C/Gas 3. Grease and line two 20cm loose-bottomed cake tins with greaseproof paper.
2. Sift together the flour, baking powder, bicarbonate of soda, spices and salt into a large bowl and set aside.
3. In a separate large bowl, beat together the sugar and butter until pale and fluffy, then beat in the eggs, banana, buttermilk and vanilla extract. Fold in the sifted flour mixture, a little at a time, then fold in the pecans.
4. Spoon half the cake mixture into each prepared cake tin, spreading the mixture out gently with a spatula or the back of a spoon. Place the cake tins into the oven and bake for about 30–40 minutes, or until a skewer inserted into the middle of the cake comes out clean. Remove from the oven and allow to sit for 10 minutes before carefully turning out on to a wire rack to cool.

5. While the cakes are baking, make the coconut frosting. Beat together the sugar and butter until creamy and fluffy. Whisk in the cream cheese until thick and smooth, but be careful not to over whip it as it can turn runny very quickly. Fold in the coconut syrup and toasted desiccated coconut and chill in the fridge for 30 minutes.
6. Once the banana cakes have completely cooled, level off their tops so that they are even. Generously spread the frosting over the top of each cake, then sandwich the cakes together.
7. Slice generously and serve, or store in an airtight container, in the fridge, for up to 3 days, allowing the cake to reach room temperature before enjoying it.

Bounty Bites

MAKES 24 BALLS

Condensed milk and coconut (grated, desiccated or creamed) are two ingredients that appear in many of our Caribbean treats. This afternoon nibble or post-dinner confection uses both ingredients and is then dunked in chocolate – the only thing that could make that duo even better! Wait for that oh-so-familiar chocolate-bar taste to set in on the first bite . . .

TIME: 25 MINUTES PREP + OVERNIGHT CHILLING + 5 MINUTES COOKING + 2 HOURS SETTING

150g desiccated coconut
180g condensed milk
225g good-quality milk chocolate, broken into small pieces
225g good-quality dark chocolate (70% cocoa solids), broken into small pieces
sea salt

1. Line a large baking sheet with cling film.
2. In a large bowl, stir together the desiccated coconut and condensed milk until mixed.
3. Using a spoon, scoop some of the coconut mixture and use another spoon to mould it into a 2.5cm-diameter ball. Place the ball on to the prepared baking tray and continue to

mould more balls until you have used up all the coconut mixture. Carefully cover the baking sheet with more cling film and pop into the fridge overnight, until firm.

4. When the coconut balls are firm, remove the cling film covering them then carefully lift the cling film they are sitting on (with the balls still on top) from the baking sheet and set aside. Line the baking sheet with a fresh piece of cling film.
5. To make the milk chocolate coating, melt the milk chocolate with a pinch of salt in a small heatproof bowl placed over a small pan of simmering water, making sure that the bottom of the bowl doesn't come into contact with the water. Stir the chocolate occasionally with a heatproof spatula. As soon as the chocolate has completely melted, carefully remove the bowl from the pan and set it down on a heatproof surface.
6. Using two spoons, take a coconut ball and roll it around in the chocolate until fully coated. Place it on to the prepared cling-film-covered baking sheet and continue with half of the remaining balls.
7. Repeat steps 5 and 6 above to cover the remaining balls in the dark chocolate.
8. Leave the Bounty Bites in a cool place to set, about 2 hours. Once set, carefully pop them all together into a small bowl, or on to a plate, to serve. Alternatively, store in an airtight container in the fridge for up to 7 days.

Coconut Sweet Bread

MAKES ONE LOAF (SERVES ABOUT 6)

I think every bread bin should have a constant supply of this crumbly coconut bread. It obviously has some sweetness, but at the same time doesn't really fall into the dessert category, so I never feel too bad about indulging in a slice in the mornings, toasted (obviously), with a generous slather of butter melting into it, the way it should be eaten! It is also the perfect addition to afternoon tea – try it with clotted cream and jam to shake up the traditional spread. It is rather crumbly, so you have an excuse to slice it generously!

TIME: 10 MINUTES PREP + 50–60 MINUTES COOKING

225g self-raising flour
100g desiccated coconut
90g soft light brown sugar
1 heaped tsp baking powder
½ tsp ground cinnamon
½ tsp ground nutmeg
¼ tsp ground cloves
100g mixed raisins/currants/sultanas
pinch of sea salt
1 small free-range egg, beaten

140ml coconut milk
60g unsalted butter, melted and cooled, plus a little for greasing the loaf tin
1½ tsp Angostura bitters
1 tsp vanilla essence

1. Pre-heat the oven to 160°C/Gas 3. Grease a 21 x 11 x 4.5cm loaf tin with a little butter.
2. In a large bowl, whisk together the flour, desiccated coconut, sugar, baking powder and spices until evenly mixed.
3. In another bowl, whisk together the egg, coconut milk, melted butter, Angostura bitters and vanilla extract until mixed.
4. Little by little fold the liquid mixture into the dry mixture, along with the raisins, until there are no dry patches left and the batter is like cookie dough but don't overmix it or you will end up with a tough bread.
5. Pour the batter into the loaf tin and pop in the oven for about 50-60 minutes, until golden and a skewer inserted into the centre of the loaf comes out clean.
6. Carefully turn the loaf out on to a wire rack to cool. Store in an airtight container and eat within 3 days.

Cardamom Chilli Truffles

MAKES ABOUT 20 TRUFFLES

These special little spheres of indulgence are delicately dusted with exotic cardamom and chilli, bringing out a wonderful warmth in the chocolate. Use the best quality chocolate you can find as it really is the key ingredient. I love the heat that builds at the end, but feel free to use a little less chilli if you prefer. I like to pop some of these truffles into clear, cellophane bags, tie them up with string and label them with luggage tags to offer as gifts. They never cease to please.

TIME: 15 MINUTES PREP + 2 MINUTES COOKING + 3 HOURS COOLING

150g good-quality dark chocolate (70% cocoa solids), broken into small pieces
pinch of sea salt
150g double cream
60g light muscovado sugar
1½ tsp ground green cardamom
¼ tsp chilli powder
a small dash of good-quality dark rum
30g cocoa, for dusting
scant pinch of chilli flakes, roughly chopped

1. Place the chocolate and a pinch of sea salt in a large bowl and set aside.
2. In a small saucepan, bring the cream, sugar, cardamom, chilli powder and rum to the boil and stir for a minute. Remove the pan from the heat and allow to cool for a couple of minutes.
3. Pour the cream mixture over the chocolate pieces and use a spatula to stir continuously until the chocolate has completely melted and you have a smooth and glossy ganache. Let the ganache cool to room temperature then place in the fridge for 3 hours, until set.
4. Line a baking sheet with greaseproof paper and place the cocoa in a small bowl. Remove the chilled ganache from the fridge. Scoop a teaspoonful of the ganache, dust your fingertips in cocoa and use them to quickly roll the ganache into a cocoa-covered ball. Pop the truffle on the greaseproof paper and continue with the remainder of the ganache. Garnish with a scant pinch of chilli flakes.
5. Serve immediately. Store in the fridge in an airtight container for up to 3 days or freeze them and defrost as needed.

DRINK UP

Jungle Smoothie

SERVES 4-6

Green smoothies are great because not only can they really boost you on the way to your five-a-day but they also retain the all-important fibre that is sometimes lost in the juicing process. This energy-boosting recipe is perfect for those, like my husband, who run a mile at the thought of drinking veg, because the cocoa nibs (high in antioxidants), chilled banana (a good source of energy and high in potassium), cinnamon and vanilla make this taste like a milkshake! Also lurking is virgin coconut oil, which is high in lauric acid and is antiviral, antibacterial and a great immune-system booster. I call this a shh . . . moothie because that milkshake taste secretly masks a whole manner of goodness with the only give away being that jungle green colour.

TIME: 10 MINUTES PREP

- 125g coconut-milk yoghurt, or Greek yoghurt
- 700ml chilled milk (you can use any type: dairy, soya, coconut or almond)
- 1 chilled, ripe avocado (refrigerate overnight), peeled and stone removed, roughly chopped
- 2 tbsp cocoa nibs
- 160g spinach, washed
- 4 medium bananas, peeled and roughly chopped

¾ tsp ground cinnamon
½ tsp good-quality vanilla extract
4 tsp clear honey

1. In a blender, blitz together the yoghurt, milk and avocado until smooth. Add the cocoa nibs and blend for a further few minutes, until smooth. (The cocoa nibs will break up into tiny pieces rather than fully dissolve.)
2. Blend in the spinach, then the banana and add the cinnamon and vanilla extract.
3. Finally, add honey to taste (you may prefer to use more, less or even none at all) and give a final blitz to mix. Serve immediately.

Peanut Punch

SERVES 4-6

If you like peanut butter, you will love this! In the past, Peanut Punch has been advertised as a drink 'for potency' and as a 'man's drink'. I'm not exactly sure why that is, because I believe it appeals to a full spectrum of folk (I loved it as a kid and love it as an adult!). It hints of sweetness, but actually isn't all that sweet: it is well spiced, a tad aromatic and a touch salty. You can also add a little rum, or vodka, to make it a little more naughty . . .

TIME: 5 MINUTES PREP

1.2 litres whole milk
2 ¼ tbsp malted milk powder
225g smooth, unsweetened peanut butter
3 liberal splashes of Angostura bitters
¾ tsp ground cinnamon
¾ tsp grated fresh nutmeg
pinch of sea salt
3-9 tbsp condensed milk

1. In a small bowl stir together 1½ tablespoons of the milk with the malted milk powder until you have a smooth paste.
2. Pour into a blender and add all the remaining ingredients except the condensed milk. Blitz until smooth.
3. Sweeten to taste by stirring in the condensed milk.

Watermelon Tamarind Iced Tea

SERVES 6–10

We drink a lot of tea in the Caribbean, and actually hot drinks are generally all referred to as 'tea' (yes, it does get a bit confusing when tea can also mean either hot chocolate or coffee!). Funnily enough, though, we don't drink as much iced tea as you might expect. This refreshing afternoon cooler is something a little different to the usual lemon iced tea, with a lovely sour tang from the tamarind balancing the sweet lusciousness of the watermelon. Use as much or as little sugar syrup as you desire.

TIME: 15 MINUTES PREP + 2 HOURS CHILLING

4 black tea bags
1 litre boiling water
750g seeded watermelon flesh
2 tbsp tamarind concentrate, or paste
2 tbsp sugar syrup, plus extra to taste
4 mint sprigs
ice, to serve
lime wedges, to decorate

1. Put the tea bags into a large jug, pour over the boiling water and leave to infuse for 20 minutes. Squeeze the tea bags, then remove them and leave the tea to cool.

2. In the meantime, purée the watermelon flesh by blitzing with a stick blender until smooth, then strain to remove any remaining lumps.
3. Stir the tamarind concentrate, sugar syrup and puréed watermelon into the cooled tea, until well combined. Add the mint sprigs and chill for a couple of hours. (It will keep in the fridge for up to 2 days.)
4. Stir well before serving over ice and garnish with a lime wedge.

Ginger Beer Cordial

SERVES 8–12

This delightfully fiery beverage is so much more homely and tasty than the sugary, canned stuff that you can buy in supermarkets. It reminds me of lounging around on the porch in Trinidad on a stiflingly hot afternoon, fanning away mosquitos. Every sip of this stuff was ambrosial! Having it in a cordial form makes it so versatile, especially if you freeze it as ice cubes. You can drink it cold, served over ice (and with a little golden rum) or stirred into cocktails. Enjoy it as a hot tea in the afternoon with a slice of lemon, or drizzle it over desserts and fruit salads.

TIME: 10 MINUTES PREP + 3 DAYS 'DEVELOPING'

1kg fresh root ginger, peeled and grated
6 cloves
1.6 litres freshly boiled water
about 480ml sugar syrup
juice of 1 lime
some generous splashes of Angostura bitters
lime wedges, to garnish
mint leaves, to garnish

1. Place the ginger, cloves and freshly boiled water into a large, sterilised bottle (or divide between two bottles) and leave to cool to room temperature with the lid off. Once

cooled, pop the lid on, give the bottle a good shake and allow to steep in the fridge for 3 days.
2. Strain the soaked ginger through a sieve, reserving the liquid only and squeezing out any excess liquid from the ginger. Pour the liquid into another large, sterilised bottle and add the sugar syrup, lime juice and Angostura bitters.
3. To serve, pour 75–100ml of the Ginger Beer Cordial into a glass and top with 75ml of still, sparkling or boiling water. Top with a wedge of lime and a few mint leaves.
4. Keep the Ginger Beer Cordial in the fridge for up to 2 weeks, or freeze, in batches or as ice cubes, for up to 2 months.

Rum Punch

SERVES 6–8

You will find rum punch throughout the Caribbean. It is usually pre-mixed and kept in an old, large plastic bottle behind the bar, and will undoubtedly be firewater strong! When we moved to the UK, Ma was renowned for her punches at parties we had. Anytime I asked her how she made it, she would reply 'one of sour, two of sweet, three of strong, four of weak'. The recipe below kind of fits this. Feel free to add any other fruit juice you like: I am a big fan of using fresh juices as the flavour is that little bit more zesty.

TIME: 5 MINUTES PREP

500ml good-quality dark rum
150ml sugar syrup
150ml freshly squeezed lime juice
100ml freshly squeezed grapefruit juice
500ml freshly squeezed orange juice
1½ tbsp Angostura bitters
1 tbsp grenadine syrup

To serve
ice cubes
grated fresh nutmeg
orange slices
maraschino cherries

1. Combine all the punch ingredients in a large jug, stirring well. Add more sugar syrup, if desired.
2. Strain the punch to remove any pulp and serve over ice (or chilled) with a generous sprinkle of grated nutmeg and a speared cocktail stick of sliced orange and a maraschino cherry.

Piña Colada

SERVES 4–6

I am a little embarrassed to admit that this cocktail, along with a Whisky Sour (just to show my macho side!), is one of my favourite drinks. I think the ice cream is great and makes it a super quick-and-easy alternative to a dessert during the summer (and even winter) months.

TIME: 10 MINUTES PREP

120ml good-quality dark rum
200ml coconut cream
150g canned, drained pineapple chunks
100ml pineapple juice
½ tsp ground nutmeg
few dashes of Angostura bitters
5 large scoops of vanilla ice cream

To serve
crushed ice
pineapple leaves
maraschino cherries
grated nutmeg

1. In a blender, blitz together all the piña colada ingredients, except the ice cream, until smooth.

2. Add the ice cream and blitz for a few seconds, until mixed.
3. Divide between tall cocktail glasses of crushed ice and decorate each glass with a couple of pineapple leaves, a maraschino cherry and a sprinkle of nutmeg.

Turmeric 'Tea'

SERVES 4-6

Whilst turmeric has been notching up the column inches recently with its impressive health benefits – including its anti-inflammatory, anti-fungal and antibacterial properties – my Aunty Sita has been making this turmeric-based chai for years. This earthy, warming and aromatic drink is the perfect nightcap, as well as being good for you. Turmeric does stain, so try to peel, chop and handle it in a contained area, and use lemon juice to clean up any staining afterwards.

TIME: 5 MINUTES PREP + 20 MINUTES COOKING

- 1 litre milk (dairy, almond, soya or any other sort you fancy)
- 20g turmeric root, peeled and roughly chopped
- 6 cloves
- 8 tbsp coconut cream
- 2 tsp ground cinnamon
- 1–1½ tsp ground green cardamom
- ½ tsp allspice
- 4–6 tsp honey, depending on how sweet you want it

1. In a blender, blitz the milk and the turmeric for a few minutes, until blended.
2. Put all the ingredients into a small saucepan (just use 4 teaspoons of the honey to begin with) and warm on a medium heat for 20 minutes, stirring regularly. Try not to let it boil.
3. Strain then serve, adding a little more honey if you want a sweeter drink.

FOR THE
LARDER

Grapefruit Curd

MAKES ENOUGH TO FILL ONE 450g JAR

This recipe was a pleasant accident (I used grapefruit in my lemon curd – don't ask me how!) and is like a spreadable version of a favourite breakfast – sugar-sprinkled grapefruit. As the saying goes, you eat with your eyes first – that creamy pinky-amber sunset colour just makes me want to dive straight in and it looks fantastic next to the marmalade on the breakfast table – but don't worry if you only have yellow grapefruits, as it will still taste incredible. Slather on to toast, cakes and pancakes or use it to make tarts and other desserts.

TIME: 5 MINUTES PREP + 35 MINUTES COOKING + 10 MINUTES COOLING

zest and juice of 1 pink grapefruit
200g caster sugar
100g unsalted butter, diced
8 free-range egg yolks, beaten
1 level tsp cornflour, made into a smooth paste with a couple of drops of water
¼ tsp allspice

1. Place a large heatproof bowl over a pan of simmering water on a medium heat, ensuring that the bottom of the bowl is not in contact with the water. Add the grapefruit zest and

juice, sugar and butter to the bowl and stir until the butter has melted.

2. Add the egg yolks and cornflour paste and continue to whisk until the curd thickens to a custard-like consistency and the mixture feels heavy on the whisk, about 35 minutes. (Don't worry that it doesn't yet have a curd consistency, it will thicken up as it cools.)
3. Remove from the heat and continue to whisk now and again whilst the curd cools. Stir in the allspice.
4. After the curd has cooled for about 10 minutes, pour it into a sterilised jar, filling it right to the top and pop the lid on. Leave to cool completely, then store in the fridge and use within a month.

Sunshine Granola

SERVES 4–8 (FILLS A 1-LITRE JAR)

I am of a generation that grew up at a time when cereals were the breakfast food of choice for kids. And they were always sugary, brightly coloured and faux-marshmallow-based. When we moved to the UK, Ma succeeded in shifting us to a healthier granola-based morning meal, with a dollop of yoghurt and a splash of milk, of which I still often partake at weekends. I find that many store-bought varieties can be very high in added sugars, and expensive. This recipe uses naturally sweet fruits of the Caribbean baked in an incredibly addictive, spiced passion fruit honey. Chop and change the dried fruit as you wish. It stores well, is cheap to make and can even be a lovely gift, especially when presented in a ribbon-tied jar.

TIME: 10 MINUTES PREP + 50 MINUTES COOKING + 10 MINUTES COOLING

140g jumbo rolled oats
40g pumpkin seeds
80g cashew nuts, roughly chopped
1 large free-range egg white
40g desiccated coconut
40g dried mango slices, chopped into thirds
40g dried pineapple chunks

40g banana chips, broken into bite-sized pieces
40g prunes, chopped into bite-sized chunks

For the passion fruit honey
2 passion fruits, pulp and seeds only
170g clear honey
½ tbsp olive oil
4 tsp ground cinnamon
pinch of ground allspice
pinch of sea salt

1. Pre-heat the oven to 150°C/Gas 2.
2. In a large bowl, mix together all the ingredients for the passion fruit honey.
3. Add the oats, pumpkin seeds and cashew nuts to the passion fruit honey and stir well to coat all the ingredients.
4. In a separate bowl, beat the egg white until frothy and fold into the wet granola mix.
5. Pour the wet granola out on to a large baking tray and spread out evenly. Bake for 30 minutes, taking the tray out to gently stir twice during this time (trying to avoid breaking up any clumps).
6. Add the desiccated coconut and bake for a further 20 minutes, until golden brown, gently stirring halfway through.
7. Remove the tray from the oven and let the granola crisp up as it cools to room temperature.
8. Mix in the dried fruit and serve with yoghurt (or other good dairy-free coconut-milk yoghurt), plain yoghurt, or chilled milk, or store in an airtight container for up to 2 weeks.

Spiced Chocolate

**MAKES 15–18 SERVINGS
(1 HEAPED TABLESPOON PER 150ml MILK SERVING)**

I'm a little obsessed with liquid chocolate, hot or cold: I probably knock back four glasses or mugs of it a week. Here's my special chocolate recipe that hints of balmy, spice-enveloped evenings. You can enjoy it iced too: first mix a heaped tablespoon of powder with 2 teaspoons of iced milk until you form a paste, then add the remaining iced milk. Otherwise, make the paste with cold milk, heat the remaining milk until hot and stir into the paste. It's especially delicious if you dollop over a large spoon of double cream – go on, you know you want to! Spiced bliss in a cup.

TIME: 5 MINUTES PREP + 2 HOURS FREEZING

125g good-quality plain chocolate (70% cocoa solids)
75g good-quality milk chocolate
60g good-quality cocoa powder
40g icing sugar
30g cornflour
25g malted milk powder
2 tsp ground cinnamon
1 tsp ground ginger

½ tsp sea salt
½ tsp cayenne pepper
scant pinch of ground cloves

1. Put the plain and milk chocolate in the freezer for a couple of hours then finely chop.
2. Put all the ingredients in an airtight jar, stir well with a fork to ensure everything is mixed then close the lid and give the jar a good shake.
3. Store in a cool, dark place for up to 3 months.

Condensed Milk

MAKES ABOUT 350 ml

You may have noticed how frequently condensed milk comes to play in Caribbean sweets. When I was a child, we very rarely had fresh milk, so condensed milk (and sometimes evaporated milk) would be used to sweeten teas, coffees and desserts. When we moved to the UK, my Ma would buy cans of the stuff, but, actually, I didn't realise how simple – and cheap – it is to make your own, and tailor its viscosity and sweetness to your taste. Sometimes I sprinkle in a little ground green cardamom, ground cloves and cinnamon to make a spiced version. This is great in warm drinks, spread on hot toast, used in tarts and drizzled over pastries, pancakes, French toast and desserts.

TIME: 10 MINUTES PREP

125g skimmed milk powder
125g granulated sugar
90ml boiling water
55g unsalted butter, melted
a couple of drops of good-quality vanilla extract

1. Pop all the ingredients into a blender and blitz until the sugar has dissolved and everything is well mixed and smooth. If you would like to make the condensed milk less thick, just add a few more tablespoons of boiling water.
2. Pour into sterilised jars, allow to cool and store in the fridge for up to a week.

Jars

Pumpkin Jam

MAKES ENOUGH TO FILL TWO 450g JARS

I am a big fan of this thick, meaty jam smothered on hot buttered currant bread or even toasted plain bread that won't mask its delicate taste. The addition of these earthy spices makes it reminiscent of pumpkin pie at first and then the subtle, distinctive pumpkin flavour lingers on your tongue at the end.

TIME: 5 MINUTES PREP + 45 MINUTES COOKING

800g pumpkin flesh, cut into 2.5cm chunks
1 tsp ground allspice
1 tsp ground cinnamon
½ tsp ground ginger
zest of 1 orange
680g jam sugar

1. Chill a saucer in the fridge (to test the jam setting point).
2. Cook the pumpkin in a large saucepan of boiling water for about 15–20 minutes until tender.
3. Drain well then blitz the pumpkin with a stick blender until puréed.
4. Return the puréed pumpkin to the large pan and mix in the spices and the orange zest. Add the sugar and 120ml water, stir and heat gently on the lowest setting to dissolve the

sugar, stirring regularly, for about 10–15 minutes. Make sure that you don't boil the mixture at this point though.

5. When all the sugar has dissolved, turn the heat up to high and bring to a rolling boil for about 5–10 minutes until the jam reaches setting point. Test this by placing a teaspoon of jam on the chilled saucer. Pop it back in the fridge for a minute to cool then give it a little nudge with your finger; if the surface crinkles, then it has set. If not, then continue to boil the jam for a further 5 minutes or so and test again.

6. Once it has reached setting point, remove from the heat, leave the jam to cool for about 10 minutes, then pour into two sterilised jars, filling them right up to the top and pop the lids on. Leave to cool completely, then store in the fridge and use within 1 month. If you seal the sterilised jars and store them in a cool, dark cupboard, the jam will keep, unopened for up to a year.

Yellow Pepper Jam

MAKES ABOUT 500ml

If a jar of mango chutney and a jar of chilli jam were to meet, fall in love and have a baby, this ruby-studded beauty would be it! If you want to amp up the heat, add more Scotch bonnet pepper. The sweetness of the yellow pepper and mango complement that 'pow' just perfectly. Enjoy it with fritters, savoury canapés and snacks, cheese, cold cuts and sandwiches. I make jars and jars of this at Christmas: it is a fabulous gift to give (and receive).

TIME: 10 MINUTES PREP + 20 MINUTES COOKING

- 2 soft, ripe mangoes (about 400g flesh), peeled, stoned and roughly chopped
- 4 medium yellow peppers, seeded and roughly chopped
- 1 Scotch bonnet pepper, seeded and roughly chopped (use disposable gloves)
- 2 garlic cloves, crushed
- ½ thumb-sized piece of fresh root ginger, peeled and roughly chopped
- ½ tsp Angostura bitters
- ¼ tsp ground allspice
- 100ml cider vinegar
- 400g jam sugar

1. Chill a small saucer in the fridge (to test the jam setting point).
2. Pop the mango, yellow pepper, Scotch bonnet, garlic, ginger, Angostura bitters and allspice into a food processor and blitz until you get a smoothish paste.
3. In a large saucepan on a low heat, swirl (don't stir) the vinegar and sugar by moving the pan in a circular motion, until the sugar has dissolved, about 5–10 minutes. Don't let the mixture boil.
4. Add the pepper–mango paste, giving the pan a swirl, and bring the mixture up to a boil. Keep the mixture on a rolling boil for about 10 minutes. To test whether the jam has set, place a teaspoon of jam on the chilled saucer. Pop it back in the fridge for a minute to cool then give it a little nudge with your finger; if the surface crinkles, then it has set. If not, then continue to boil the jam for a further 5 minutes or so and test again.
5. Once the jam has reached setting point, remove the pan from the heat and allow it to cool a little, for about 10 minutes. At this stage you can give the jam a proper stir, distributing all the loveliness throughout.
6. Pour the jam into sterilised jars, filling them right up to the top and pop the lid on. Leave to cool completely, then store in the fridge and use within a month. If you seal the sterilised jar and store it in a cool, dark cupboard, it will keep, unopened, for up to a year.

Pepper Sauce

MAKES ABOUT 500ml

If I were to recommend one recipe from this book for you to start with, it would be this one. Without a doubt, this hot sauce is the mother of all Caribbean condiments and tends to be a permanent feature on the table for all three meals of the day (as well as those in between!) and it crops up a lot in this book. We refer to Scotch bonnets, bird's eye chillies and other spicy chillies as 'peppers' rather than chillies. Although it is undeniably hot, the beauty of this sauce is that it is also extremely flavoursome and a couple of drops here and there really add something special to certain dishes. If you want to go for a 'blow-your-head-off' heat, feel free to amp up the Scotch bonnet. Don't worry if the colour changes every time you make a batch of this, it all depends on what colour Scotch bonnets you use-whatever colour, it will taste just as good! And if you really have a death wish, you could try taking a leaf from my Uncle Derek's book: he snacks on Scotch bonnets (seeds and all) dipped into pepper sauce! To make your Pepper Sauce last, don't stick metal cutlery into it, use plastic or wooden spoons.

TIME: 10 MINUTES PREP + 10 MINUTES COOKING + 2 DAYS 'DEVELOPING

1 lime
12 medium-sized Scotch bonnet peppers (to make it super

hot use 20 peppers), stems removed, roughly chopped (use disposable gloves)
15g coriander leaves
cloves of 1½ garlic bulbs, peeled
150ml white wine vinegar
1½ heaped tbsp caster sugar
1 tbsp American mustard
1 small thumb-sized piece of fresh root ginger, peeled and roughly chopped
½ green, unripe (firm to touch) papaya, peeled, stoned, and roughly chopped
sea salt and freshly ground black pepper

1. Put the lime in a small saucepan and cover with cold salted water. Bring to the boil and cook the lime until soft and tender, about 10–15 minutes. Set aside to cool.
2. In the meantime, place all the other ingredients, except the salt and pepper, into a blender and blitz until smooth.
3. Finely chop the lime (keeping the peel on), discarding any seeds, and stir into the other ingredients.
4. Decant the Pepper Sauce into a sterilised bottle, pop the lid on and leave to 'develop' flavour for 2 days, then season to taste with sea salt and freshly ground pepper (it will take a lot of salt!) and give the bottle a good shake to distribute the seasoning.
5. Store in the fridge for up to 6 months (don't worry about any discolouration over time).

Molasses & Rum Barbecue Sauce

MAKES ABOUT 500ml

This aromatic, sticky-sweet sauce will really set off your barbecued meats, fish and veggies a treat, whether you use it as a marinade, glaze, or simply smother it on at the end. It's also great for jazzing up baked beans and brunches.

TIME: 10 MINUTES PREP + 35 MINUTES COOKING

3 tbsp olive oil
200g molasses sugar
1 onion, roughly chopped
6 garlic cloves, crushed
2 bay leaves
1 tsp fennel seeds, crushed
1 tsp ground coriander
1 tsp ground ginger
1 tsp cayenne pepper
1 x 400g can chopped tomatoes
6 tbsp cider vinegar
200g molasses sugar
2 tbsp Worcestershire sauce
2 tbsp soy sauce
2 tbsp English mustard
1 tsp Angostura bitters
juice of 1 lime

100ml good-quality dark rum
1 tbsp tomato purée
zest of ½ orange
sea salt and freshly ground black pepper

1. Heat the oil in a medium-sized sauce pan. Add the onion and soften with a small pinch of salt, stirring often, for about 5 minutes.
2. Add the garlic, bay leaves and spices and stir for 30 seconds, until the aromas are released.
3. Add the remaining ingredients and bring to the boil, then reduce the heat and simmer, with the lid off, for 30 minutes, stirring regularly, until thick.
4. Use a stick blender to blitz the sauce until smooth. Season to taste. If the consistency of the Barbecue Sauce is too loose, pour it back into the pan and simmer on a low heat, stirring regularly, until it has thickened. Remember that as it cools it will thicken a little more.
5. Pour the Barbecue Sauce into a sterilised bottle, pop the lid on and store in the fridge for up to 6 months.

Pineapple Ketchup

MAKES ABOUT 400ml

My love of condiments definitely comes from my Caribbean heritage. We love to have an array of sauces, dips and chutneys to enhance the flavours of our meals. This pineapple ketchup is rich, exotic and spicy (in flavour, not heat). Although there are a lot of ingredients here, this ketchup is really easy to make and so worth it. It works really well with barbecued meats and, in fact, steps in whenever you might have used tomato ketchup. It also has a particularly high 'chip-dunkability' factor!

TIME: 15 MINUTES PREP + 1 HOUR COOKING

5 tbsp olive oil
4 medium-sized onions, roughly chopped
2 celery sticks, roughly chopped
6 garlic cloves, roughly chopped
4 bay leaves
½ small red chilli, seeded and roughly chopped
2 cinnamon sticks, roughly chopped
2 tsp freshly ground black pepper
2 tsp ground coriander
2 tsp ground allspice
2 tsp yellow mustard seeds, ground
¾ tsp ground nutmeg
¾ tsp ground ginger

¾ tsp ground green cardamom
¾ tsp ground cloves
4 ripe, medium pineapples (about 2.6kg of flesh), peeled, cored and cut into small chunks
400ml white wine vinegar
120g caster sugar
sea salt

1. Heat the oil in a large saucepan on a low heat. Add the onion, celery and a small pinch of salt, stirring often, until soft, about 5 minutes.
2. Add the garlic, bay leaves, chilli and dried spices and stir for a further minute, until the aroma hits you.
3. Add the pineapple, vinegar and sugar and bring to the boil, then reduce the heat and simmer, with the lid off, for about 20 minutes, stirring now and again.
4. Using a handheld blender, blitz the mixture until smooth, then strain into a clean pan, using the back of a spoon to push all the lovely flavours through.
5. Boil on a high heat until thickened and reduced to a ketchup consistency, about 30-40 minutes, stirring regularly. Remember that as it cools it will thicken a little more. Season to taste.
6. Decant the ketchup into a sterilised bottle, pop the lid on and store in the fridge for up to 6 months.

Cocktail Sauce

SERVES 4-6

At oyster stalls in Trinidad, vendors pop shucked, raw oysters in shot glasses and pour over cocktail sauce and you neck them back in the usual fashion, having as many shots as you fancy, paying as you go. This sauce, which should always be served chilled, is more akin to a ceviche sauce than to a typical prawn cocktail one. This particular recipe is based on one that my Uncle Michael makes and that Ma drinks like water! Not only does it work well with freshly shucked oysters in shot glasses, it is also great to use as a dip for cooked prawns and other chilled seafood as well as big cubes of cucumber. You can also use it as a killer base, along with tomato juice and a little Worcestershire sauce, for a mean Bloody Mary or Bloody Pirate (with rum instead of vodka).

TIME: 5 MINUTES PREP

- 2 ripe tomatoes, seeded and diced
- ⅛ Scotch bonnet pepper, seeded
- juice from ½ lime
- 2 tbsp chopped coriander leaves
- 1 large garlic clove, peeled and crushed
- 1 tbsp tomato ketchup
- ½ tsp light brown sugar
- ½ tsp soy sauce
- sea salt and freshly ground black pepper

1. Pop all the ingredients, except the salt and pepper, into a blender, add 100ml water and blitz until smooth. Season to taste.
2. Store in a clean bottle or jar, in the fridge, for up to 5 days.

Sauce Creole

SERVES 4-6

This sauce is packed with a lot of ingredients that work together to create a tangy, spicy, sweet-and-savoury sauce that you can spoon over grilled or pan-fried fish and meats, bake with vegetables or spoon over mashed potato and meatballs. You can also blitz it until smooth and serve with spaghetti and a little grated cheese. It is so versatile and the flavour really rocks! I always keep an emergency jar of it in the fridge for when I need to throw together a quick meal at the last minute. For a quick and tasty snack, try spreading it over large tortilla wraps with a little cheese, onion, pepper and ham, then grilling until the cheese has melted.

TIME: 15 MINUTES PREP + 20 MINUTES COOKING

6 tbsp olive oil
1 large onion, finely chopped
1 celery stick, finely chopped
2 red peppers, seeded and finely chopped
3 garlic cloves, crushed
1 small red chilli, seeded, and finely chopped
3 tsp dried thyme leaves
3 tsp dried oregano
1 ½ tsp cayenne pepper
4 x 400g cans cherry tomatoes

3 tbsp chicken (or vegetable) stock
½ tbsp sherry vinegar
1 tsp Worcestershire sauce
3 tbsp tomato purée
25g butter
1 tbsp caster sugar
sea salt and freshly ground black pepper

1. Heat the oil in a large saucepan on a medium heat. Add the onion, celery and peppers and soften with a small pinch of salt, stirring often, for about 5 minutes.
2. Add the garlic, chilli, herbs and cayenne pepper and cook for about 30 seconds, stirring regularly, until the aroma is released.
3. Add the tinned tomatoes, stock, vinegar, Worcestershire Sauce, tomato purée, butter and sugar. Bring the sauce to the boil, then simmer, with the lid slightly off, for 15 minutes, stirring occasionally until reduced and thickened. Season to taste.
4. You can either blitz the sauce with a stick blender until thick and smooth or leave it chunky.
5. Pour into clean bottles, leave to cool and store in the fridge for up to 5 days, or freeze, in batches, for up to 2 weeks, defrosting before warming through.

Chow-Chow

MAKES ENOUGH TO FILL TWO 500ml JARS

This pickle, which is similar to a piccalilli, was traditionally brought out with the Christmas ham, but it has gradually found its way to hot dogs and burgers, cold cuts and cheese lunches and other relish-imperative meals. I love Chow-Chow with cheese, boiled eggs and a salad of leaves, radish, celery, cucumber and tomato – a variation on a ploughman's lunch, if you like.

TIME: 10 MINUTES PREP + 20 MINUTES COOKING + 2 WEEKS 'DEVELOPING'

60g cauliflower, broken into small florets
60g carrots, scrubbed and chopped into 2cm chunks
60g red pepper, seeded and cut into 2cm chunks
60g onion, finely chopped
60g unripe, green (hard) papaya, peeled, flesh cut into 1cm chunks
60g cucumber, cut into 2cm chunks
1 celery stick, cut into 1cm slices
60g soft light brown sugar
20g cornflour
2 tsp English mustard powder
2 tsp yellow mustard seeds
1½ tsp allspice

1½ tsp ground turmeric
1½ tsp ground ginger
1 tsp ground black pepper
1 tbsp sea salt
4 garlic cloves, peeled and crushed
360ml cider vinegar

1. In a large saucepan of salted boiling water, boil the cauliflower, carrots, red pepper, onion, papaya, cucumber and celery for about 10 minutes, until tender. Drain the vegetables and papaya (emptying the water from the pan) and set aside.
2. In a small bowl, combine the sugar, cornflour, mustards, spices and salt with 60ml water. Whisk until smooth.
3. Put this mixture in the pan, add the garlic, and cook for a few minutes on a low heat, whisking continuously, until thick and paste-like.
4. Whisk the vinegar into the paste, increase the heat and bring the mixture to the boil. Finally, return the vegetables and the papaya to the pan and boil, stirring often, for about 10 minutes, until the liquid is thick and glossy.
5. Put a little Chow-Chow on to a spoon, let it cool for a couple of minutes, then taste and readjust the seasoning if necessary.
6. Pour the Chow-Chow into sterilised jars, filling them right up to the top, then pop a non-metallic or vinegar-proof lid on and leave to develop for a couple of weeks before enjoying. Once opened, store in the fridge and use within 6 months.

Marinades and Rubs

Green Seasoning

MAKES ABOUT 100 ml (ENOUGH FOR ABOUT 3-4 MEALS FOR 4)

As important as salt is in a lot of Caribbean food, especially in Trinidad, green seasoning acts like a natural flavour-enhancer. It can be used in virtually all savoury dishes, particularly with fish, meat and veg, either as a marinade or added during the cooking process, for example in stews, one pots and curries. I recommend keeping a batch in the fridge so you can add a tablespoon or so to your meals as it truly adds a bomb of flavour, whilst being versatile and subtle enough to adapt to fit the dish. It is also a great way to use up leftover or just 'past-it' herbs. Freeze in ice-cube trays and have it to hand whenever a little flavour-pop is needed.

TIME: 10 MINUTES PREP

12 tbsp roughly chopped chives
3 tbsp roughly chopped flat-leaf parsley leaves
3 tbsp roughly chopped coriander leaves
3 tbsp roughly chopped thyme leaves
4 garlic cloves, roughly chopped
juice of 1 lime
2 tbsp water
½ green chilli, seeded and roughly chopped
½ tsp sea salt
½ tsp freshly ground black pepper

1. Pop all the ingredients into a food processor and blitz until you have a smooth purée.
2. Keep in the fridge and use within 2 weeks, or portion out and freeze for up to 3 months.

Jerk Marinade

MAKES ABOUT 160ml (ENOUGH FOR ABOUT 3-4 MEALS FOR 4)

Here is a marinade that you would have (rightly) expected to see in this collection of Caribbean recipes! Its star, the mighty allspice, really shines through with the spring onions, other spices and Scotch bonnet following close behind. This jerk has a beautiful layering of flavours. Just slather it over meats, fish or vegetables, marinate overnight and bake, pan-fry, griddle or barbecue away. I sometimes add a few spoonfuls of this marinade to my Molasses and Rum Barbecue Sauce (see page 260) to make a jerk barbecue sauce for serving with meats and dunking sweet potato wedges into.

TIME: 10 MINUTES PREP + 2 MINUTES COOKING

8 tsp allspice berries
5 tsp black peppercorns
1 cinnamon stick, broken into pieces
2 tsp coriander seeds
8 spring onions, roughly chopped, bulb discarded
8 garlic cloves, peeled
1-2 Scotch bonnet peppers, seeded
8 dried bay leaves, crushed
2 tbsp demerara sugar
2 level tbsp sea salt

5 tsp thyme leaves
2 tsp grated fresh nutmeg
½ thumb-sized piece of fresh ginger, peeled and roughly chopped
3 tsp clear honey
juice of 1 lime
2 tsp olive oil
1 tsp soy sauce

1. In a frying pan on a low heat, toast the allspice berries, black peppercorns, cinnamon pieces and coriander seeds, shaking the pan often, for a couple of minutes until the aroma of the spices is released.
2. Pop the spices into a pestle and mortar and bash until everything has broken down into a grainy powder (don't worry about pieces of cinnamon: the food processor will deal with them).
3. Pop all the ingredients into the food processor and blitz until you have a smoothish paste.
4. Place in a jar and store in the fridge for up to 2 weeks, or divide into portions and freeze for up to 3 months and defrost as needed.

Adobo Spice Rub

**MAKES ENOUGH FOR 6 MEALS FOR 4
(ALLOW ROUGHLY 1 tsp RUB PER PERSON)**

'Adobo' comes from the Spanish word for marinade and was originally used to preserve meats. This is one of the quintessential Caribbean rubs and is jam-packed with flavour. The best way to use a rub is to score the meat, fish or veg with a sharp knife, coat with a little olive oil then massage the rub deep into the flesh and leave to marinate for at least six hours, and ideally overnight, before cooking. This adobo spice rub is particularly good for white, meaty fish, chicken, potato and aubergine, all cooked on a smoking hot griddle pan or barbecued and served with a light salad. Try mixing with room-temperature butter to create a flavoured butter for roasting chicken, baking veg or just spreading on to warm bread.

TIME: 5 MINUTES PREP + 2 MINUTES COOKING

1 tbsp cumin seeds
1 tsp fennel seeds
¼ tbsp black peppercorns
1½ tbsp sea salt
2 tsp oregano
½ tbsp cayenne pepper
½ tbsp paprika

1½ tsp onion powder
1½ tsp garlic powder
¼ tsp ground turmeric

1. In a frying pan on a low heat, toast the cumin seeds, fennel seeds and black peppercorns for a couple of minutes, shaking the pan regularly, until the aroma of the spices hits you.
2. Grind the toasted seeds and peppercorns using a pestle and mortar until you have a coarse powder. Add the remaining ingredients and mix with a fork or small whisk until well combined.

Chilli–Cocoa Rub

**MAKES ENOUGH FOR 6 MEALS FOR 4
(ALLOW ROUGHLY 1 tsp RUB PER PERSON)**

Chocolate and chilli is a combination that crops up everywhere: whether in a sweet or savoury dish, it just works. This rub is all about the subtlety of the cocoa (brought out by the little sprinkle of espresso) working in harmony with the chilli and spice and is ideal for marinating pork, ribs, beef, steak, game, squash, pumpkin and sweet potato. You can also add it to a pork- or beef-based gravy, stock or even barbecue sauce, then warm through to create a chilli–cocoa sauce to accompany your meal.

TIME: 10 MINUTES PREP + 2 MINUTES COOKING

3 tbsp cocoa nibs
2 tbsp demerara sugar
½ tbsp chilli flakes
½ tbsp sea salt
½ tbsp paprika
½ tsp instant espresso powder
¼ tsp ground cinnamon
¼ tsp allspice
¼ tsp garlic granules
¼ tsp onion granules

1. Crush the cocoa nibs, demerara sugar, chilli flakes and sea salt in a pestle and mortar until reduced to a coarse powder.
2. Add the remaining ingredients and mix with a fork or small whisk until well combined.

Amchar Masala

MAKES 3 tbsp (ENOUGH FOR THE MAIN BASE FOR A CURRY FOR 4-6, A DRY RUB FOR A MEAL FOR 6-8, OR A 'FLAVOUR BOOSTER' FOR 3 MEALS FOR 6)

Amchar masala is based on an Indian spice blend that Trinis have developed into their own unique mix. It is a perfect example of how Caribbean food takes its inspiration from different regions of the world and is honed and influenced by people and produce over time into its own distinct character. The essence of this mix is earthy, toasted and warm with a gorgeous hint of aniseed. I find that it works well as the spice blend (fried with onion and garlic first) for a tomato- or coconut milk-based curry; as a dry rub (used with a little slick of oil) for roasting lamb, chicken, pork and fish; and as general flavour 'oompher' for sprinkling into stews and soups. It is also used to pickle fruits, most commonly grated green mangoes, called 'kuchela'.

TIME: 2 MINUTES PREP + 2 MINUTES COOKING

- 2 tsp cumin seeds
- 1 tsp fenugreek seeds
- 1 tsp fennel seeds
- 1 tsp black mustard seeds
- 1 tsp coriander seeds
- 1 tsp black peppercorns
- ¼ tsp ground ginger

1. In a large frying pan on a medium heat, toast all the seeds and the peppercorns for about 2 minutes until darkened (but not burnt) and the aroma of the spices is strongly released.
2. Crush the seeds and peppercorns in a pestle and mortar until reduced to a coarse powder then add the ground ginger and mix with a fork until well combined.
3. Transfer to an airtight jar and leave to cool to room temperature before closing.

Rum Raisins

MAKES ENOUGH TO FILL ABOUT TWO 450ml JARS

Here is a quick 'cheat' recipe based on something Father Louie once taught me in Virgin Gorda. Calling it a 'cheat' does not make it any less tasty, but it does make whipping up a rum-and-raisin ice cream as simple as loading a few tablespoons of this super treat over a scoop of vanilla ice cream. I've also discovered that it is great to fold into whipped cream and serve with simple sponges and cakes or dipped into molten chocolate. This is all on the assumption that you can resist eating them straight from the jar though! It may be a test of patience, but the developing time is key to the raisins becoming 'plumpscious' with a warm, scrummy mellowness.

TIME: 5 MINUTES PREP + 5 DAYS 'DEVELOPING'

250g raisins
150ml good-quality dark rum
100ml sugar syrup

1. Put all the ingredients into a bowl and stir to combine.
2. Divide between sterilised jam jars, ensuring that there is enough space left in the jars to give the raisins a shake.
3. Leave to 'develop' in the fridge for 5 days, shaking the jars twice a day to redistribute the raisins in the jars.
4. The Rum Raisins will keep in the fridge for up to 3 months.

Acknowledgements

How special to have a 10 year reissue of a book that truly changed my life. With a career that began with my bi-weekly Caribbean supper clubs, sharing my food with new people, telling stories about the heritage of the dishes, making them in my own style and being a general feeder, to cooking these dishes on television for a whole different audience and now having a breakfast show with my name on it 10 years on. There are so many people to thank!

Firstly, to the entire team on the book, my incredible literary agent, Antony Topping, who really believed in it then and still believes in my Caribbean food now, to Muna, Imogen, Kris, Lucy, Pene, Poppy, Faith and Isla, and George and Jo, this, my first ever book baby was made possible only because of the collaborative effort of all of you. And to Lindsey who so wonderfully resurrected this spanking new version, 10 years on. Thank you!

To everyone, (and there are so many of you!) who has given me an opportunity to showcase what I could do, who has believed in me and give me a chance, initially at the time when Caribbean food was a little unchartered, to even now, in a climate where there is uncertainty, I am honoured you were certain with me. To Amanda Ross for giving me my first chance to showcase my way of Caribbean food and my lovely commissioner, Leanne Clarke, who keeps championing me, thank you.

To 'my' people: my beautiful Ben who has been with me from the inception of this culinary adventure, who has stirred a few dishes for me, picked up a few forgotten ingredients, inspired some new recipes, eaten all the others and helped me balance it all with our utterly delicious babies, Miles, Eliot and Hazel (who have all stuck their fingers in various plates of food!). My Trini (and Trini outpost in Canada/UK) family, all of who have provided, stories and culinary secrets, who have fed me the best food I have ever tasted, especially Auntie Sita, who I spent time with in Trinidad, talking and cooking some of these dishes and who is a continuous fountain of knowledge, even from across the Globe. And of course, Ma and Pa, to whom this book is dedicated, all of the recipes have woven through it my childhood and a mountain of memories with Rhea and Ash, how lucky we are! Thank you.

And finally, to the audience of people reading this book, coming to my supper clubs, watching me cooking on TV, searching my recipes on the web and continually being hungry for more, thank you. I wouldn't be here 10 years on without you. Save some space, there is more to come!

Index

Adobo spice rub 275–6
aïoli 128–9
allspice
    Banana tarte tatin 183–4
    Carrot & lentils 50–1
    Chilli-cocoa rub 277–8
    Chow-chow 268–9
    Chunky monkey cake 217–19
    Coconut chicken 'rundown' 101–2
    Coconut rice & peas 143–5
    Grapefruit curd 245–6
    Pineapple ketchup 262–3
    Pumpkin jam 254–5
    Pumpkin lava cake & black pepper cardamom custard 185–7
    Red bean & spinach mac 'n' cheese 94–5
    Sunshine granola 247–8
    Turmeric 'tea' 240–1
    Yellow pepper jam 256–7
almonds
    Black cake 214–16
    'Pasteles' 109–12
amchar masala 279–80
    Coconut chicken 'rundown' 101–2
    Curried crab & dumplings 91–3
    Curried duck 84–6
    'Paradise' prawns 30–1
Angostura bitters
    Banana tarte tatin 183–4
    Black cake 214–16
    Coconut sweet bread 222–3
    Crab backs 54–5
    Ginger beer cordial 234–5
    Lamb pepperpot 96–8
    Molasses and rum barbecue sauce 260–1
    Peanut punch 231
    Pelau 81–3
    Piña colada 238–9
    Rum punch 236–7
    Yellow pepper jam 256–7
apple: Green mango & sour apple chow 71–2
aubergine
    Aubergine croquettes 35–7
    Choka 17–19
    Lamb pepperpot 96–8
avocado
    Bag-baked sea bass & black bean salsa 113–15
    Buljol butties 128–9
    Jungle smoothie 229–30
    Zaboca gazpacho 69–70
    Zaboca on crab biscoti 21–2

bacon
    Bacon-studded pumpkin talkari 152–3
    Doved peas 156–7
    'Pasteles' 109–12
    Shellfish chowder 103–5
Bag-baked sea bass & black bean salsa 113–15
Baigan choka 17–19
'Bake & shark' 125–7
Baked eggs creole 130–1
Baked split peas 25–6
banana
    Banana cake 217–19
    Banana tarte tatin 183–4
    Chunky monkey cake 217–19
    Jungle smoothie 229–30
    Mashed green bananas 150–1
    Salt beef oil down 99–100
    Smashed banana pancakes 193–4
    Sunshine granola 247–8

beef: Jamaican beef patties 121–4
beetroot: Tamarind-dressed sweet potato & beetroot salad 58–60
black beans
  Bag-baked sea bass & black bean salsa 113–15
  Shrimp & black bean fritters with tamarind dip 32–4
Black cake 214–16
black pudding: Scallop, puddin' & sour 47–9
Blackened corn salad 73–5
bone marrow; 'Pasteles' 109–12
Bounty bites 220–1
Buccaneer's shortbread 209–11
Buljol butties 128–9
Buss-up shut 148–9
buttermilk
  Buttermilk fried chicken, biscuits & milk gravy 116–20
  Chunky monkey cake 217–19
  Cornmeal baked okra 23–3
butternut squash
  Coconut chicken 'rundown' 101–2
  Geera pork chops with citrus garlic gremolata 87–90

cabbage
  Corned beef & cabbage 132–3
  Pineapple & peanut slaw 154–5
Callaloo 45–6
Candied ginger 177–9
Cardamon chilli truffles 224–5
cauliflower
  Cauliflower & coconut soup with lime & garlic croutons 52–3
  Chow-chow 268–9
celery
  Cauliflower & coconut soup with lime & garlic croutons 52–3
  Chow-chow 268–9
  Corn soup 61–3
  Pineapple ketchup 262–3

Salt beef oil down 99–100
Sauce creole 266–7
Shellfish chowder 103–5
cheese
  Cheese 'rotsies' 38–40
  Red bean & spinach mac 'n' cheese 94–5
cherry brandy
  Black cake 214–16
chicken
  Buttermilk fried chicken, biscuits & milk gravy 116–20
  Coconut chicken 'rundown' 101–2
  Pelau 81–3
chickpeas
  Curried duck 84–6
  Tamarind-dressed sweet potato & beetroot salad 58–60
chilli
  Bag-baked sea bass & black bean salsa 113–15
  Baked split peas 25–6
  Callaloo 45–6
  Carrot & lentils 50–1
  Cheese 'rotsies' 38–40
  Chilli-cocoa rub 277–8
  Cocktail sauce 264–5
  Coconut chicken 'rundown' 101–2
  Coconut rice & peas 143–5
  Cornmeal baked okra 23–4
  Crab backs 54–5
  Curried crab & dumplings 91–3
  Curried duck 84–6
  Geera pork chops with citrus garlic gremolata 87–90
  Green seasoning 271–2
  Jerk marinade 273–4
  Kale bhaji 158–9
  Lamb pepperpot 96–8
  Mock conch salad 76–7
  Pelau 81–3
  Pepper sauce 258–9
  Pineapple & peanut slaw 154–5

Pineapple chilli crème brûlée 172–4
Pineapple ketchup 262–3
Roasted coconut & cucumber salad 64
Salt beef oil down 99–100
Sauce creole 266–7
Scallop, puddin' & sour 47–9
Shrimp & black bean fritters with tamarind dip 32–4
Spice-crust & lemon 'aïoli' 27–9
Yellow pepper jam 256–7
Zaboca on crab biscotti 21–2

chives
  Blackened corn salad 73–5
  Buljol butties 128–9
  Callaloo 45–6
  Cheese 'rotsies' 38–40
  Corn soup 61–3
  Crab backs 54–5
  Curried crab & dumplings 91–3
  Curried duck 84–6
  Green seasoning 271–2
  Jamaican beef patties 121–4
  Lamb pepperpot 96–8
  Mashed green bamnanas 150–1
  'Pasteles' 109–12
  Pelau 81–3
  Salt beef oil down 99–100
  Zaboca gazpacho 69–70

chocolate/chocolate chips
  Bounty bites 220–1
  Buccaneer's shortbread 209–11
  Cardamon chilli truffles 224–5
  Double ginger chocolate mousse 177–9
  Smashed banana pancakes 193–4
  Spiced chocolate 249–50

Choka 17–19
Chow-chow 268–9
Chunky monkey cake 217–19
Cocktail sauce 264–5

cocoa nibs
  Chilli-cocoa rub 277–8
  Double ginger chocolate mousse 177–9
  Jungle smoothie 229–30

coconut
  Bounty bites 220–1
  Buccaneer's shortbread 209–11
  Chunky monkey cake 217–19
  Coconut chicken 'rundown' 101–2
  Coconut rice & peas 143–5
  Coconut soufflé & hot buttered rum 165–7
  Coconut sweet bread 222–3
  Roasted coconut & cucumber salad 64
  Sunshine granola 247–8
  Sweet potato pone 207–8

coconut cream
  Coconut rice & peas 143–5
  Kale bhaji 158–9
  Pelau 81–3
  Piña colada 238–9
  Snow cones 195–6
  Turmeric 'tea' 240–1

coconut milk
  Callaloo 45–6
  Cauliflower & coconut soup with lime & garlic croutons 52–3
  Coconut chicken 'rundown' 101–2
  Coconut rice & peas 143–5
  Coconut soufflé & hot buttered rum 165–7
  Coconut sweet bread 222–3
  Curried crab & dumplings 91–3
  Pineapple fritters with lime caramel & rum whipped cream 190–2
  Salt beef oil down 99–100
  Sweet potato pone 207–8

coconut oil
  Bag-baked sea bass & black bean salsa 113–15
  Cauliflower & coconut soup with lime & garlic croutons 52–3
  Coconut rice & peas 143–5
  'Paradise' prawns 30–1
  Salt, lime & coriander popcorn 20
  Salted tamarind caramel sundae 180–2
  Smashed banana pancakes 193–4

coconut syrup: Coconut soufflé & hot buttered rum 165-7
Condensed milk 251-2
coriander
  Amchar masala 279-80
  Bag-baked sea bass & black bean salsa 113-15
  'Bake & shark' 125-7
  Blackened corn salad 73-5
  Carrot & lentils 50-1
  Cauliflower & coconut soup with lime & garlic croutons 52-3
  Cheese 'rotsies' 38-40
  Choka 17-19
  Cocktail sauce 264-5
  Cou-cou & fish 134-7
  Curried duck 84-6
  Geera pork chops with citrus garlic gremolata 87-90
  Green mango & sour apple chow 71-2
  Green seasoning 271-2
  Jerk marinade 273-4
  Mock conch salad 76-7
  Molasses and rum barbecue sauce 260-1
  'Paradise' prawns 30-1
  Pepper sauce 258-9
  Pineapple & peanut slaw 154-5
  Pineapple ketchup 262-3
  Roasted coconut & cucumber salad 64
  Salt, lime & coriander popcorn 20
  Shrimp & black bean fritters with tamarind dip 32-4
  Spice-crust & lemon 'aïoli' 27-9
  Tamarind-dressed sweet potato & beetroot salad 58-60
  Zaboca gazpacho 69-70
corn kernels/ears of
  Blackened corn salad 73-5
  Corn soup 61-3
Corn soup 61-3
Corned beef & cabbage 132-3
cornflour
  Buttermilk fried chicken, biscuits & milk gravy 116-20
  Chow-chow 268-9
  Coconut soufflé & hot buttered rum 165-7
  Grapefruit curd 245-6
  Passion lime meringue pie 197-200
  Pineapple fritters with lime caramel & rum whipped cream 190-2
  Spice-crust & lemon 'aïoli' 27-9
  Spiced chocolate 249-50
cornmeal
  Cornmeal baked okra 23-4
  Cou-cou & fish 134-7
  'Pasteles' 109-12
  Sweet potato pone 207-8
Cou-cou & fish 134-7
Crab backs 54-5
crabmeat/claws
  Crab backs 54-5
  Curried crab & dumplings 91-3
  Zaboca on crab biscotti 21-2
cream cheese
  Chunky monkey cake 217-19
  Peanut butter cheesecake with grape jelly 201-3
Crispy chickpeas 58-60
cucumber
  Chow-chow 268-9
  Roasted coconut & cucumber salad 64
cumin
  Adobo spice rub 275-6
  Amchar masala 279-80
  Bacon-studded pumpkin talkari 152-3
  Carrot & lentils 50-1
  Cauliflower & coconut soup with lime & garlic croutons 52-3
  Cornmeal baked okra 23-4
  Curried crab & dumplings 91-3
  Geera pork chops with citrus garlic gremolata 87-90
  Spice-crust & lemon 'aïoli' 27-9
  Spiced sweet potato wedges 146-7

Curried crab & dumplings 91–3
Curried duck 84–6

Dark chocolate and ginger
   mousse 177–9
Double ginger chocolate mousse 177–9
Doved peas 156–7
duck: Curried duck 84–6

eggs
   Aubergine croquettes 35–7
   'Bake & shark' 125–7
   Baked eggs creole 130–1
   Black cake 214–16
   Buttermilk fried chicken, biscuits &
      milk gravy 116–20
   Chunky monkey cake 217–19
   Coconut soufflé & hot buttered rum
      165–7
   Coconut sweet bread 222–3
   Corned beef & cabbage 132–3
   Double ginger chocolate
      mousse 177–9
   Grapefruit curd 245–6
   Jamaican beef patties 121–4
   Passion lime meringue pie 197–200
   Pineapple chilli crème brûlée 172–4
   Pineapple fritters with lime caramel
      & rum whipped cream 190–2
   Pumpkin lava cake & black pepper
      cardamom custard 185–7
   Shrimp & black bean fritters with
      tamarind dip 32–4
   Smashed banana pancakes 193–4
   Sunshine granola 247–8
   Zaboca on crab biscotti 21–2

fennel
   Adobo spice rub 275–6
   Geera pork chops with citrus garlic
      gremolata 87–90
   Molasses & rum barbecue sauce
      260–1

fenugreek
   Amchar masala 279–80
   Geera pork chops with citrus garlic
      gremolata 87–90
fish *see also* individual entries
   'Bake & shark' 125–7
   Buljol butties 128–9
   Cou-cou & fish 134–7
   Fried fish 134–7
fried bakes 141–2
   'Bake & shark' 125–7
   Buljol butties 128–9
   'Fry bodi' 160

Geera pork chops with citrus garlic
   gremolata 87–90
ginger
   Amchar masala 279–80
   Carrot & lentils 50–1
   Chow-chow 268–9
   Coconut chicken 'rundown' 101–2
   Curried crab & dumplings 91–3
   Curried duck 84–6
   Double ginger chocolate mousse 177–9
   Ginger beer cordial 234–5
   Ginger-citrus dressing 56–7
   Ginger-dressed tomato, orange & red
      onion salad 56–7
   Jerk marinade 273–4
   Molasses and rum barbecue sauce
      260–1
   Pelau 81–3
   Pepper sauce 258–9
   Pineapple ketchup 262–3
   Pumpkin lava cake & black pepper
      cardamom custard 185–7
   Spiced chocolate 249–50
   Sweet potato pone 207–8
   Yellow pepper jam 256–7
grapefruit
   Grapefruit curd 245–6
   Mock conch salad 76–7
   Rum punch 236–7

grapes: Peanut butter cheesecake with grape jelly 201-3
Green mango & sour apple chow 71-2
green pepper: Shellfish chowder 103-5
green seasoning 271-2
   'Bake & shark' 125-7
   Corned beef & cabbage 132-3
   Cou-cou & fish 134-7
   Geera pork chops with citrus garlic gremolata 87-90
   Pelau 81-3
grenadine
   Grenadine orange salad 170-1
   Snow cones 195-6
gungo peas
   Doved peas 156-7
   Pelau 81-3

ham
   Callaloo 45-6
   Doved peas 156-7
   Pelau 81-3
honey
   Carrot & lentils 50-1
   Ginger-dressed tomato, orange & red onion salad 56-7
   Jerk marinade 273-4
   Jungle smoothie 229-30
   Sunshine granola 247-8
   Tamarind-dressed sweet potato & beetroot salad 58-60
   Turmeric 'tea' 240-1

Ice cream 180-2

Jamaican beef patties 121-4
jerk marinade 273-4
   Jerk pulled pork & watermelon salad 65-8
Jerk pulled pork & watermelon salad 65-8
Jungle smoothie 229-30

Kale bhaji 158-9
kidney beans
   Coconut rice & peas 143-5
   Red bean & spinach mac 'n' cheese 94-5

lamb: Lamb pepperpot 96-8
lentils (puy): Carrot & lentils 50-1

macaroni: Red bean & spinach mac 'n' cheese 94-5
mango
   Bag-baked sea bass & black bean salsa 113-15
   Green mango & sour apple chow 71-2
   Mango mojito granita 168-9
   Mango sour 47-9
   Scallop, puddin' & sour 47-9
   Snow cones 195-6
   Sunshine granola 247-8
   Yellow pepper jam 256-7
Mashed green bamnanas 150-1
mayonnaise
   'Bake & shark' 125-7
   Buljol butties 128-9
   Pineapple & peanut slaw 154-5
   Spice-crust & lemon 'aïoli' 27-9
mint
   Ginger beer cordial 234-5
   Grenadine orange salad 170-1
   Mango mojito granita 168-9
   Poached pawpaw & vanilla whip 175-6
   Watermelon tamarind iced tea 232-3
   Zaboca gazpacho 69-70
Mock conch salad 76-7
molasses and rum barbecue sauce 260-1
   Red bean & spinach mac 'n' cheese 94-5
mussels: Shellfish chowder 103-5

nuts
   Carrot & lentils 50-1
   Chunky monkey cake 217-19
   Coconut rice & peas 143-5

Peanut butter cheesecake with grape
  jelly 201–3
Pineapple & peanut slaw 154–5
Salt & spice brittle 212–13
Salted tamarind caramel sundae 180–2
Sunshine granola 247–8

okra
  Callaloo 45–6
  Cornmeal baked okra 23–4
  Cou-cou & fish 134–7
olive oil
  Adobo spice rub 275–6
  Bacon-studded pumpkin talkari 152–3
  Baked eggs creole 130–1
  Baked split peas 25–6
  Blackened corn salad 73–4
  Buljol butties 128–9
  Buss-up shut 148–9
  Callaloo 45–6
  Carrot & lentils 50–1
  Cauliflower & coconut soup with lime
    & garlic croutons 52–3
  Cheese 'rotsies' 38–40
  Choka 17–19
  Coconut chicken 'rundown' 101–2
  Coconut rice & peas 143–5
  Corned beef & cabbage 132–3
  Cornmeal baked okra 23–4
  Cou-cou fish 134–7
  Curried crab & dumplings 91–3
  Curried duck 84–6
  Fried bakes 141–2
  'Fry bodi' 160
  Geera pork chops with citrus garlic
    gremolata 87–9
  Ginger-dressed tomato, orange & red
    onion salad 56–7
  Green mango & sour apple chow 71–2
  Jamaican beef patties 121–4
  Jerk marinade 273–4
  Kale bhaji 158–9
  Lamb pepperpot 96–8

Mashed green bananas 150–1
Mock conch salad 76–7
Molasses & rum barbecue sauce 260–1
'Paradise' prawns 30–1
'Pasteles' 109–12
Pelau 81–3
Pineapple ketchup 262–3
Salt beef oil down 99–100
Sauce creole 266–7
Scallop, puddin' & sour 47–9
Shellfish chowder 103–5
Spliced sweet potato wedges 146–7
Sunshine granola 247–8
Tamarind-dressed sweet potato &
  beetroot salad 58–60
Zaboca gazpacho 69–70
Zaboca on crab biscoti 21–2
olives: 'Pasteles' 109–12
orange
  Ginger-dressed tomato, orange & red
    onion salad 56–7
  Grenadine orange salad 170–1
  Jerk pulled pork & watermelon salad
    65–8
  Lamb pepperpot 96–8
  Mock conch salad 76–7
  Molasses and rum barbecue sauce 260–1
  Pumpkin jam 254–5
  Rum punch 236–7
  Shrimp & black bean fritters with
    tamarind dip 32–4
  Tamarind-dressed sweet potato &
    beetroot salad 58–60
oregano
  Pineapple & peanut slaw 154–5
  Sauce creole 266–7
  Shellfish chowder 103–5

pancetta: Scallop, puddin' & sour 47–9
papaya
  Chow-chow 268–9
  Pepper sauce 258–9
  Poached pawpaw & vanilla whip 175–6

'Paradise' prawns 30–1
parsley
   Aubergine croquettes 35–7
   Blackened corn salad 73–5
   Callaloo 45–6
   Choka 17–19
   Corn soup 61–3
   Crab backs 54–5
   Curried crab & dumplings 91–3
   Geera pork chops with citrus garlic gremolata 87–90
   Green seasoning 271–2
   'Pasteles' 109–12
passion fruit
   Passion lime meringue pie 197–200
   Snow cones 195–6
   Sunshine granola 247–8
'Pasteles' 109–12
Peanut butter cheesecake with grape jelly 201–3
Peanut punch 231
Pelau 81–3
pepper sauce 258–9
   'Bake & shark' 125–7
   Buljol butties 128–9
   Corned beef & cabbage 132–3
   Doved peas 156–7
   Green mango & sour apple chow 71–2
   Jamaican beef patties 121–4
   'Pasteles' 109–12
   Shellfish chowder 103–5
   Shrimp & black bean fritters with tamarind dip 32–4
Piña colada 238–9
pineapple
   Blackened corn salad 73–5
   Piña colada 238–9
   Pineapple & peanut slaw 154–5
   Pineapple chilli crème brûlée 172–4
   Pineapple fritters with lime caramel & rum whipped cream 190–2
   Pineapple ketchup 262–3
   Sunshine granola 247–8

Poached pawpaw & vanilla whip 175–6
polenta
   'Pasteles' 109–12
   Polenta dumplings 91–3
pomegranate
   Coconut rice & peas 143–5
   Grenadine orange salad 170–1
popping corn
   Salt, lime & coriander popcorn 20
   Salted tamarind caramel sundae 180–2
pork
   Geera pork chops with citrus garlic gremolata 87–90
   Jerk pulled pork & watermelon salad 65–8
potatoes
   Bag-baked sea bass & black bean salsa 113–15
   Cheese 'rotsies' 38–40
   Curried duck 84–6
   Lamb pepperpot 96–8
   Shellfish chowder 103–5
prawns
   'Paradise' prawns 30–1
   Shellfish chowder 103–5
   Shrimp & black bean fritters with tamarind dip 32–4
prunes
   Black cake 214–16
   Sunshine granola 247–8
pumpkin
   Bacon-studded pumpkin talkari 152–3
   Pumpkin jam 254–5
   Pumpkin lava cake & black pepper cardamom custard 185–7
   Salt & spice brittle 212–13
   Sunshine granola 247–8

Ragu 109–12
Red bean & spinach mac 'n' cheese 94–5
red pepper
   Blackened corn salad 73–5

Cheese 'rotsies' 38–40
Chow-chow 268–9
Corned beef & cabbage 132–3
'Pasteles' 109–12
Pelau 81–3
Sauce creole 266–7
rice: Corned beef & cabbage 132–3
rocket
    Scallop, puddin' & sour 47–9
    Tamarind-dressed sweet potato & beetroot salad 58–60
Roasted coconut & cucumber salad 64
rum
    Black cake 214–16
    Buccaneer's shortbread 209–11
    Cardamom chilli truffles 224–5
    Coconut soufflé & hot buttered rum 165–7
    Curried duck 84–6
    Mango mojito granita 168–9
    Molasses and rum barbecue sauce 260–1
    Piña colada 238–9
    Pineapple fritters with lime caramel & rum whipped cream 190–2
    Rum punch 236–7
    Rum raisins 28–1
    Watermelon sherbet 188–9

Salad 47–9
Salad dressing 71–2
salad leaves: Scallop, puddin' & sour 47–9
Salt & spice brittle 212–13
Salt beef oil down 99–100
Salt, lime & coriander popcorn 20
Salted tamarind caramel sundae 180–2
sauce creole 266–7
    Baked eggs creole 130–1
    Cou-cou & fish 134–7
Scallop, puddin' & sour 47–9
Scotch bonnet *see* chilli
sea bass
    Bag-baked sea bass & black bean salsa 113–15
    Mock conch salad 76–7
Shellfish chowder 103–5
Shrimp & black bean fritters with tamarind dip 32–4
Smashed banana pancakes 193–4
Snow cones 195–6
Spice-crust & lemon 'aïoli' 27–9
Spiced chocolate 249–50
Spiced coconut shortbread 209–11
Spiced sweet potato wedges 146–7
spinach
    Baked eggs creole 130–1
    Callaloo 45–6
    Jungle smoothie 229–30
    Red bean & spinach mac 'n' cheese 94–5
    Salt beef oil down 99–100
split peas
    Baked split peas 25–6
    Corn soup 61–3
squid: Spice-crust & lemon 'aïoli' 27–9
steak: 'Pasteles' 109–12
string beans: 'Fry bodi' 160
Sunshine granola 247–8
sweet potato
    Spiced sweet potato wedges 146–7
    Sweet potato pone 207–8
    Tamarind-dressed sweet potato & beetroot salad 58–60
Syrup ('milk', 'red', 'golden') 195–6

tamarind concentrate/paste
    Salted tamarind caramel sundae 180–2
    Shrimp & black bean fritters with tamarind dip 32–4
    Watermelon tamarind iced tea 232–3
Tamarind sauce 125–7
Tamarind-dressed sweet potato & beetroot salad 58–60
Tamarind dressing 58–60

thyme
- Callaloo 45-6
- Coconut chicken 'rundown' 101-2
- Cornmeal baked okra 23-4
- Curried crab & dumplings 91-3
- Curried duck 84-6
- Doved peas 156-7
- Green seasoning 271-2
- Jamaican beef patties 121-4
- Jerk marinade 273-4
- Lamb pepperpot 96-8
- 'Pasteles' 109-12
- Red bean & spinach mac 'n' cheese 94-5
- Salt beef oil down 99-100
- Sauce creole 266-7
- Shellfish chowder 103-5

tomato
- 'Bake & shark' 125-7
- Buljol butties 128-9
- Choka 17-19
- Cocktail sauce 264-5
- Curried crab & dumplings 91-3
- 'Fry bodi' 160
- Geera pork chops with citrus garlic gremolata 87-90
- Ginger-dressed tomato, orange & red onion salad 56-7
- Mock conch salad 76-7
- Molasses and rum barbecue sauce 260-1
- Sauce creole 266-7
- Shellfish chowder 103-5
- Tomato choka 17-19

turmeric
- Adobo spice rub 275-6
- Coconut chicken 'rundown' 101-2
- Chow-chow 268-9
- Curried crab & dumplings 91-3
- Jamaican beef patties 121-4
- 'Paradise' prawns 30-1
- Salt beef oil down 99-100
- Turmeric 'tea' 240-1

Vanilla whip 175-6

watercress: Jerk pulled pork & watermelon salad 65-8

watermelon
- Jerk pulled pork & watermelon salad 65-8
- Snow cones 195-6
- Watermelon tamarind iced tea 232-3
- Watermelon sherbet 188-9

wine: 'Pasteles' 109-12

yellow/orange pepper
- Buljol butties 128-9
- Crab backs 54-5
- Geera pork chops with citrus garlic gremolata 87-90
- Mock conch salad 76-7
- Yellow pepper jam 256-7

yoghurt
- Cauliflower & coconut soup with lime & garlic croutons 52-3
- Jungle smoothie 229-30
- Poached pawpaw & vanilla whip 175-6
- Smashed banana pancakes 193-4

Zaboca gazpacho 69-70
Zaboca on crab biscotti 21-2

RAISING READERS
Books Build Bright Futures

Dear Reader,

We'd love your attention for one more page to tell you about the crisis in children's reading, and what we can all do.

Studies have shown that reading for fun is the **single biggest predictor of a child's future life chances** – more than family circumstance, parents' educational background or income. It improves academic results, mental health, wealth, communication skills, ambition and happiness.[1]

The number of children reading for fun is in rapid decline. Young people have a lot of competition for their time. In 2024, 1 in 10 children and young people in the UK aged 5 to 18 did not own a single book at home.[2]

Hachette works extensively with schools, libraries and literacy charities, but here are some ways we can all raise more readers:

- Reading to children for just 10 minutes a day makes a difference
- Don't give up if children aren't regular readers – there will be books for them!
- Visit bookshops and libraries to get recommendations
- Encourage them to listen to audiobooks
- Support school libraries
- Give books as gifts

There's a lot more information about how to encourage children to read on our website: **www.RaisingReaders.co.uk**

Thank you for reading.

---

[1] OECD, '21st-Century Readers: Developing Literacy Skills in a Digital World', 2021, https://www.oecd.org/en/publications/21st-century-readers_a83d84cb-en.html

[2] National Literacy Trust, 'Book Ownership in 2024', November 2024, https://literacytrust.org.uk/research-services/research-reports/book-ownership-in-2024